# Critical Squares

# Critical Squares
## Games of Critical Thinking and Understanding

Shari Tishman
Project Zero
Harvard Graduate School of Education

Albert Andrade
Project Zero
Harvard Graduate School of Education

With Foreword by
David Perkins

1997
Teacher Ideas Press
a Division of
Libraries Unlimited, Inc.
Englewood, Colorado

TEACHER IDEAS PRESS
a Division of
Libraries Unlimited, Inc.
P.O. Box 6633
Englewood, CO 80155-6633
1-800-237-6124
www.lu.com


Constance Hardesty, *Project Editor*
Jane Olivier, *Production Coordinator*
Rick Frye, *Design and Layout*

**Library of Congress Cataloging-in-Publication Data**

Tishman, Shari.
    Critical squares : games of critical thinking and understanding /
Shari Tishman, Albert Andrade ; with foreword by David Perkins.
    xv, 125 p. 22x28 cm.
    ISBN 1-56308-490-2
    1. Educational games.   2. Critical thinking--Study and teaching.
I. Andrade, Albert.   II. Title.
LB1029.G3T47   1997
371.33'7--dc21                                      97-4225
                                                        CIP

# Contents

## 3  The Whyzit Cube Game

## 4  Causal Tic-Tac-Toe

## 5  The Connection Cube Game

## 6 The Reflection Cube Game

# Foreword

If you used this book's Starting Block game (chapter 1) on the topic of intelligence, one square would tell you to invent a pair of difficult questions about the topic. Two challenging questions might be What is intelligence? and Where is intelligence?

We have all heard too much about the first one, and most of us are pretty tired of answers that talk only about IQ. The second one is much more interesting. Most of us take it for granted that intelligence is in the head, buried somewhere in the neurochemistry of the brain and the good management of the mind. But a provocative contemporary position says something quite different: Intelligence is *distributed.* Our intelligence, in the sense of how well we function as thinking and understanding organisms, spreads out from the mind to include physical, social, and symbolic support systems. We operate more intelligently because we make use of things like notepads and computers; because we think together with other people; and because we employ language, mathematics, and other symbol systems to guide and focus our thinking and understanding.

Distributed intelligence is the perfect theme to bear in mind while exploring *Critical Squares,* a set of materials and activities that amounts to a celebration of the concept. All the activities depend on physical things to support them—the cubes and tic-tac-toe diagrams as well as notepads. All the activities depend on social interaction, as groups of students gather to roll the cubes and vie with one another to fill out the tic-tac-toe squares. Finally, language is the central symbol system, the ordinary language of everyday questioning occasionally enriched with the language of thinking, for instance, the distinction between sufficient and possible causes, the idea of brainstorming, the use of comparison and contrast, or the articulation of purposes.

By now it must be clear that the question Where is intelligence? has something to do with What is intelligence? If drawing upon the "wheres" of physical, social, and symbolic resources allows children and adults to function more intelligently, well, this is extra intelligence in the most practical sense of the word. While, classically, intelligence is conceived as a property of the black box of our skulls, practical intelligence reaches out into the world around us, something that all too often is forgotten amid the tests and many other solo rituals of education.

With that said, it should be added that the aim of *Critical Squares* and like interventions is certainly not to equip participants with cubes and tic-tac-toe diagrams that they will carry around in their pockets for the rest of their lives. Such materials and activities capitalize upon a process recognized by the great Russian psychologist Vygotsky in his well-known *Thought and Language* (1962). Vygotsky held that children acquire a good deal of their mental skill through a process of internalization. They first achieve complex patterns of thinking and understanding in supportive social circumstances and gradually make them their own. The activities of *Critical Squares* create opportunities for children to engage in patterns of thinking they would be unlikely to attain in an unsupported setting, say reading a history book or a science book at home. Such activities facilitate the internalization of complex patterns of thinking and understanding and the development of intellectual autonomy.

However, it would be misguided to view interventions like *Critical Squares* as concerned only with a passage from externals to internals, from thinking supported by a web of physical, social, and symbolic supports to "real thinking" appropriately enthroned in the solo brain. Indeed, any such position would return us quickly to the classic picture of intelligence as a measure of how well the black box works. On the contrary, one of the most fundamental properties of the mind is that we externalize as well as internalize. Even the most sophisticated thinker readily reaches for pencil and paper, for computer or calculator, for colleagues or opponents to test ideas, for symbol systems from everyday language to chemical equations to calculus to musical notation to support the trajectory of thought and understanding.

This basic fact makes the question Where is intelligence? a tricky one to answer definitively: The resources that help to define our intelligence keep moving around. Now they are here, now they are there, rather like the bean under one or another of the carnival trickster's shells. But that is as it should be. The flexible use of resources is a hallmark of intelligent behavior. This is why I like to speak of "outsmarting IQ" by using the physical, social, and symbolic resources at hand as supportively as possible for thinking and understanding. And this is why tools like *Critical Squares* can help students to function more intelligently today and tomorrow.

David Perkins
Co-Director, Project Zero
Harvard Graduate School of Education

# Acknowledgments

Developing educational materials is seldom a solitary task, and *Critical Squares* has been immeasurably enriched by all of the educators and students who have helped us.

First of all, we are grateful for the support we received from the many teachers who helped us pilot test and refine *Critical Squares* in their classrooms. In Mattapoisett, Massachusetts, at Old Rochester Regional Junior High School, our thanks to principal Robert Gardner for his accommodating spirit and to Gary Babola for managing our visits with such élan. At Old Hammondtown Elementary School, also in Mattapoisett, we thank sixth-grade teacher Bill Spark for inviting us into his classroom to work with his students.

At Memorial Elementary School in Burlington, Massachusetts, we thank teachers Sally Rubin, Jill Nelson, and Sandy Hoy for piloting *Critical Squares* as part of their regular curriculum and for providing valuable feedback concerning both the content and administration of the games. Special thanks to Tina Grotzer of Project Zero at the Harvard Graduate School of Education for her ongoing counsel, for her expertise in causal reasoning, and for acting as liaison between us and the Burlington teachers.

Others contributed to the project as well. Thanks to teachers Danni Kleiman and Jim DellaCioppa and to principal Beth McDonald of Memorial Elementary School in Rochester, Massachusetts, for their practical input on several of the chapters and for keeping their doors open to us throughout the development of the project. We thank Muriel Croft, fifth-grade teacher at the Westport Elementary School in Westport, Massachusetts, for allowing us to pilot test several early versions of the chapters in her classroom and for her insightful critiques on subsequent drafts. Also, our thanks to Tony Melli, counselor at Westport High School, and to eighth-grade teachers Carol Michael, Mike Borges, and Leona Andrade at Westport Middle School for their seamless orchestration of our visits to their schools.

We warmly thank Dorothy MacGillivray for her technical help and fine editorial eye, especially in the later stages of the project. Many of the ideas expressed in *Critical Squares* were originally developed under a grant from the John T. and Catherine D. MacArthur Foundation. We thank the foundation for its assistance, acknowledging that the ideas expressed here do not necessarily represent those of the MacArthur Foundation.

Most importantly, of course, we would like to thank all of the students who participated in the project for their genuine effort, thoughtful comments, and patience as they worked through many earlier versions of the games. All of the sample responses in this book were generated by those students. We could not have written this book without their help.

# Introduction

It is no secret that the quality and depth of students' thinking often does not meet our expectations. As teachers, we want students to retain the information we present in our lessons. But we also want more. We want students to skillfully use that information in ways that lead to deeper, more insightful understanding and learning.

*Critical Squares* is a collection of six games that develop students' critical thinking skills and deepen their understanding of subjects and topics they are already studying. The games correspond to easy-to-recognize moments in instruction; they can be used with almost any topic in any subject at any grade level from third grade on, without major changes to curricular content or structure.

## *The* Critical Squares *Games*

There are six games in all, and each one has a format familiar to all children and adults. Four of the games have a roll-of-the-dice format, and two of the games are played like tic-tac-toe. All of the games are played by students in small cooperative groups.

Each game corresponds to an instructional opportunity that is especially rich from the standpoint of critical thinking and understanding. The games are

1.  The Starting Block is a roll-of-the-dice game that is played at the beginning of a unit or lesson to motivate students and to help them access their prior knowledge about the subject.

2.  Whatzit Tic-Tac-Toe is a game of observation and comparison that is played in the middle of a unit or lesson. Its purpose is to help students think broadly about the features of something they are studying and to critically explore these features by making guided comparisons with other things.

3.  The Whyzit Cube is also played in the middle of a unit or lesson. It can be played sequentially with Whatzit Tic-Tac-Toe, using the same topic. The purpose of the Whyzit Cube game is to help students explore the structure of a topic, concept, or object by examining its purposes and evaluating its effectiveness.

4.  Causal Tic-Tac-Toe is played in a unit or lesson when students are trying to understand the causes of something, either in the natural world (e.g., the causes of beach erosion) or in the world of human behavior (e.g., personal, literary, political, or historical events). The purpose of the game is to help students go beyond a one-dimensional, linear conception of causality and appreciate the complexity and multidimensionality of causal relationships.

5.  The Connection Cube is a roll-of-the-dice game that is played during or after a unit or lesson. It helps students to integrate new knowledge with prior knowledge and to transfer knowledge to new contexts.

6. The Reflection Cube is a roll-of-the-dice game that is played toward the end of a lesson or unit to help students reflect on and evaluate their own thinking.

## Critical Squares, *Critical Thinking, and Understanding*

*Critical Squares* encourages critical thinking and understanding in several ways. First, most of the questions in the games engage students in the active use of knowledge. This means that students are encouraged to go beyond rote learning to reflect on, evaluate, and imaginatively extend the information they are learning.

Second, three of the games—Whatzit Tic-Tac-Toe, the Whyzit Cube, and Causal Tic-Tac-Toe—encourage students to analyze and reason about topics they are studying. Reason and analysis are two areas of critical thinking that play a special role in the development of subject-matter understanding, because they enable learners to examine and evaluate the deep structure of a topic or concept.

Third, three of the games—the Starting Block, the Connection Cube, and the Reflection Cube—explicitly encourage metacognition. Metacognition means thinking about thinking, and it is widely recognized as a key component of critical thinking and intelligence. Metacognition is sometimes described as mental management because thinkers who are good at metacognition are good at managing their own thinking and learning processes. *Critical Squares* cultivates mental management by asking students to do such things as take stock of their prior knowledge of a topic before studying it, actively seek connections between what they are studying and other things they know about, and evaluate their own thinking and learning processes.

## *What Makes* Critical Squares *Different from Other Thinking Skills Approaches?*

Many efforts to cultivate thinking take a dry and technical approach. Alternatively, *Critical Squares* builds on the notion that good thinking is dispositional, that is, full of spirit and attitude. The games approach honors the spirited nature of thinking and reinforces it by engaging students in critical thinking activities that are both fun and challenging.

## *How to Get Started*

Each game is explained in a chapter that includes

a reproducible game piece

guidelines for getting started

rules of the game in poster format (for handouts or posting in a prominent place)

sample student responses and guidelines for offering constructive feedback on your students' responses

suggestions for building future lessons on the basis of what you have learned about students' thinking

To get started, all you need to do is:

1. Choose any one of the six *Critical Squares* games. (You can start anywhere. Many teachers like to start with the Starting Block.)

2. Read the first several paragraphs of the chapter you have selected to get an overview of the game and its purposes. Then, follow the simple directions for playing the game.

# The Starting Block Game

## How the Starting Block Cultivates Critical Thinking and Understanding

Too often, students begin studying a topic without preparing themselves to do their best thinking. As Socrates famously argued, it is a wise person who knows the shape of his or her ignorance. The emphasis here is on the word *shape*. Students rarely come to a learning situation without any prior thoughts or questions. The Starting Block helps students shape their lack of knowledge about a topic into an active readiness to learn.

The Starting Block encourages critical thinking and understanding in the following ways:

- **Thoughtful question-asking.** The Starting Block challenges students to articulate questions about a new topic and to go beyond the obvious to seek deep and difficult questions.

- **Making connections to prior knowledge.** The Starting Block asks students to review what they already know about a topic. Although straight recall isn't itself critical thinking, the Starting Block encourages students to go beyond recall and construct new understandings by synthesizing previously unconnected information.

- **Identifying relevance.** Too often, students are asked to accept the necessity of studying a topic without identifying for themselves reasons for studying it. The Starting Block encourages students to actively seek reasons why it might be important to study a topic.

- **Inventing learning strategies.** Good thinkers are proactive and devise strategies to advance their learning. The Starting Block challenges students to invent, on their own, steps to take to learn more about the topic they are about to study.

## When to Use the Starting Block

**Use the Starting Block when beginning a new topic or unit.**

The most common time to use the Starting Block is when beginning a new topic or unit. For example, you can use the Starting Block to begin a unit on egg incubation, the periodic table, slave narratives, modern dance, the orchestra, haiku, impressionism, the joints of the body, multiplication, the geography of southern Africa, Shakespeare, the concept of justice, pronouns, or the Industrial Revolution.

If the topic is something students already know a little bit about (joints of the body, for example), you can use the Starting Block as an introductory activity. If the topic is completely new to students (haiku, perhaps), use the starting block after students have had a lesson or two.

**Use the Starting Block in the middle of a unit to infuse energy into a topic or unit, or whenever students need a boost.**

The Starting Block is a great energizer. For example, suppose you're teaching sixth-grade geometry, and your students have been working on geometry problems for two weeks. Their learning is progressing, but their energy is flagging. "Do we really have to learn more about triangles?" they complain. Play the Starting Block Game at times like this to renew students' curiosity and to generate fresh ideas and questions.

## *Getting Started*

1. Choose a Starting Block topic. It can be virtually any topic in any subject in any grade.

2. Schedule a time for students to play the Starting Block game. Typically, teachers use the Starting Block near the beginning of a unit or topic of study. A game takes about 15 minutes to play. (See the When to Use the Starting Block Game section of this chapter for more suggestions about when to use the Starting Block.)

3. Have students work in small groups, with 3–5 students in each group. Give each group

   - a Starting Block game piece, pre-assembled, or to assemble themselves (pattern appears in figure 1.1)

   - a Response Sheet (figure 1.2)

4. Explain the rules aloud, and either post the rules where students can easily refer to them, or give each group a copy of the rules. (See figure 1.3 for rules.)

5. Remind groups to record their responses on the Response Sheet as they play the game. Collect the sheets when the groups are done. If you wish, provide written or verbal feedback using the Guidelines for Feedback in this chapter.

6. See the Where to Go from Here section of this chapter for suggestions about how to build on the Starting Block in future lessons.

**1.**

As a whole group, list as many questions as possible about this topic. Time limit: 3 minutes.

**2.**

Invent two difficult questions about this topic. Ask the player on your right for help.

**3.**

What might be the most interesting thing to learn about this topic? What might be the most boring?

**4.**

Each player in the group must list one thing they already know about this topic.

**5.**

What interesting steps could you take to learn about this topic? List at least three ideas.

**6.**

Give a few reasons why it is important to learn about this topic.

*To assemble: Cut along the solid lines, fold on the dotted lines, and tape together to form a cube.*

**Figure 1.1.** The Starting Block game piece.

# Starting Block Response Sheet

Topic: _____

Names: _____

_____

Record your responses for each roll of the Starting Block. If the same challenge is rolled twice, just add the responses to the correct column.

## Challenge 1
As a whole group, list as many questions as possible about this topic. Time limit: 3 minutes.

## Challenge 2
Invent two difficult questions about this topic. Ask the player on your right for help.

**Figure 1.2.** Starting Block Response Sheet.

## Starting Block Response Sheet (continued)

**Challenge 3**
What might be the most interesting thing to learn about this topic? What might be the most boring?

**Challenge 4**
Each player in the group must list one thing they already know about this topic.

**Figure 1.2.** Starting Block Response Sheet (continued).

## Starting Block Response Sheet (continued)

**Challenge 5**

What interesting steps could you take to learn about this topic? List at least three ideas.


**Challenge 6**

Give a few reasons why it is important to learn about this topic.


**Figure 1.2.** Starting Block Response Sheet (continued).

# *Rules of the Starting Block Game*

*For groups of 3–5 players.*

1. Players take turns rolling the die. Each player has one roll per turn. The player with the last birthday in the calendar year rolls first.

2. Roll the die and answer the thinking challenge that faces up. The player who rolls the die records his or her responses on the Starting Block Response Sheet.

3. Go around the circle twice, so each player has two turns.

4. Some questions ask the whole group to respond. For group challenges, the player who rolls the die records the group's responses on the Response Sheet.

5. Sometimes, the same thinking challenge comes up two times in a row. If this happens, the player or group must respond to the challenge again. If the challenge comes up more than two times in a row, roll the die again for a new thinking challenge.

**Figure 1.3.** Rules of the Starting Block game.

From *Critical Squares: Games of Critical Thinking and Understanding.* © 1997.
Teacher Ideas Press 1-800-237-6124.

## Sample Student Responses

Teachers know a good question when they hear one. They also know a good question can create a number of thinking and learning opportunities. Each of the Starting Block's challenges pushes students to pose the kinds of questions teachers love to hear, the kind of questions that show students are thinking critically.

Figures 1.4–1.7 provide some sample student work. The samples are drawn from real students in real classrooms. They cover four different grade levels and topics.

As you read the samples, you will probably notice that not all student responses are equally strong. Students' questions and ideas are often deep, sometimes shallow; often broad, sometimes narrow. Yet, with the few not-so-great responses, you will notice many unpolished gems—responses that show, in simple and straightforward language, how students can think critically and imaginatively about the topics they are about to study.

Read these samples to learn what to expect from your own students. You'll probably find that your students' responses to the Starting Block will be equally varied and rich.

## Guidelines for Feedback: Responding to Students' Thinking

Please don't grade students on the Starting Block. It is a game, and concern about grades can rob students' thinking of inventiveness and fun. But do provide students with feedback, either by giving them written comments on their work or by offering informal verbal advice and positive reinforcement. In fact, students will ask you for feedback, especially the first few times they play with the Starting Block. They will look to you for feedback about how well they are doing, whether their answers are "right," whether their ideas are good, and so on.

The most important point about feedback is that it should be supportively informative: Your feedback should support students' thinking by providing them with information about why, from the standpoint of critical thinking, their ideas are good or not-so-good.

To identify good ideas, look for any ideas that fall into the four areas of critical thinking and mental management:

- Asking thoughtful questions
- Making connections to prior knowledge
- Identifying relevance
- Inventing learning strategies

Following are specific things to look for in each category, along with examples from actual student responses.

## Topic: Solar system

| | |
|---|---|
| **1. As a whole group, list as many questions as possible about this topic. Time limit: 3 minutes.**<br><br>How do we know when an eclipse will happen? / Why isn't there gravity in space? / How big is the solar system? / Where does the solar system end? / Is this the only solar system? / What is an asteroid? / How come we have night and day? / Why do we have only one sun? / What is a star? / How many stars are there? / What is the sun made of? / What is a black hole? / Why don't we fall out of the sun's orbit? / Where did the solar system come from? | **2. Invent two difficult questions about this topic. Ask the player on your right for help.**<br><br>How would civilization be different if we didn't know anything about the solar system, like if we didn't know when eclipses will happen and that the earth revolves around the sun?<br><br>If the sun gives off so much light, why is it dark in space? |
| **3. What might be the most interesting thing to learn about this topic? What might be the most boring?**<br><br>The most interesting thing might be to learn about comets and meteors and what happens when they hit the earth.<br><br>The most boring thing will be to have to memorize the order of the planets and their distance from the sun. | **4. Each player in the group must list one thing they already know about this topic.**<br><br>Planets revolve around the sun.<br><br>Pluto is the farthest away from the sun.<br><br>Earth is the only planet with people on it. Maybe.<br><br>If the sun didn't exist, nothing could live.<br><br>Stars are light-years away from us.<br><br>It's hard to understand the idea of infinity in space. |
| **5. What interesting steps could you take to learn more about this topic? List at least three ideas.**<br><br>Write a letter to NASA.<br><br>Ask myself who *really* would know a lot about the solar system and then ask them.<br><br>Call a space museum and get some information.<br><br>Go to an observatory.<br><br>Watch the stars at night and keep a journal of what I see. | **6. Give a few reasons why it is important to learn about this topic.**<br><br>I have a lot of questions.<br><br>It's where we live.<br><br>I have to pass the test.<br><br>You know more when you look up at the sky at night. |

**Figure 1.4.** Fifth-grade students' responses to a Starting Block game about the solar system.

## Topic: Geometry

| | |
|---|---|
| **1. As a whole group, list as many questions as possible about this topic. Time limit: 3 minutes.**<br><br>What is a right angle? / Why do people use degrees to measure angles? / How many different shapes are there? / Why is geometry part of math class? / Who invented geometry? / Can a circle be more than 360 degrees? / What is the name of a shape with 20 sides? / How can I draw three-dimensional shapes? / What is the difference between geometry and trigonometry? / What will we learn in high school geometry that we won't learn here? / How can I memorize all the shapes faster? / How did the ancient civilizations figure out geometry? | **2. Invent two difficult questions about this topic. Ask the player on your right for help.**<br><br>What is the purpose of geometry?<br><br>Is it possible to build anything without using geometry? |
| **3. What might be the most interesting thing to learn about this topic? What might be the most boring?**<br><br>An interesting thing to learn would be how geometry is used in everyday life. The most boring to do would be measuring angles.<br><br>The most interesting thing to learn would be how people used geometry to build stuff in ancient times before geometry was invented. A boring thing to learn is the names of all the different kinds of shapes. | **4. Each player in the group must list one thing they already know about this topic.**<br><br>A circle has no angles.<br><br>A decagon has 10 sides and 10 angles.<br><br>Some shapes get their names from the number of sides they have.<br><br>Lines and points are part of geometry.<br><br>A protractor is used to measure angles.<br><br>It's an important part of math. |
| **5. What interesting steps could you take to learn more about this topic? List at least three ideas.**<br><br>Look at an "old" test.<br><br>Interview people who use geometry in their work. Maybe an architect.<br><br>Think harder and do extra homework.<br><br>Decide exactly what I want to find out about geometry first.<br><br>Become a math major when you get to college.<br><br>Get a computer program to help you out. | **6. Give a few reasons why it is important to learn about this topic.**<br><br>Everything is made up of shapes.<br><br>I'll get a good grade in math.<br><br>It will help me understand geometry when I'm in high school.<br><br>We wouldn't be able to measure things. |

**Figure 1.5.** Sixth-grade students' responses to a Starting Block game about geometry.

## Topic: U.S. presidency

| | |
|---|---|
| **1. As a whole group, list as many questions as possible about this topic. Time limit: 3 minutes.**<br><br>Who does the president answer to? / What can the president do? / What *can't* the president do? / How many votes does the president need to get elected? / Can anyone *really* be president? / Why haven't we had any women presidents? / How much does the president get paid? / What happens if the president dies? / Who was our best president? / How many presidents were assassinated? / Who gives the president advice? / How many presidents have we had? / What's the difference between a Republican and Democratic president? / What can we do if we don't like what the president does? | **2. Invent two difficult questions about this topic. Ask the player on your right for help.**<br><br>How can a president represent a country that has so many different cultures living here?<br><br>Would it be possible to keep a democracy that does not have a president running it? |
| **3. What might be the most interesting thing to learn about this topic? What might be the most boring?**<br><br>The most interesting thing would be to find out about the neat things a president can do. The most boring thing would be to learn all the dates and stuff.<br><br>It would be interesting to learn about what he does all day to make his decisions. It would be boring to learn all the names of the presidents we've had.<br><br>I'd like to learn more about the presidents as people, not just what they did. | **4. Each player in the group must list one thing they already know about this topic.**<br><br>The president can choose judges.<br><br>The president decides if we'll fight in wars.<br><br>The president runs the country.<br><br>The president is elected for four years and can be re-elected.<br><br>A lot of politics is involved in getting elected president. |
| **5. What interesting steps could you take to learn more about this topic? List at least three ideas.**<br><br>Watch the news.<br><br>Read the paper more often.<br><br>Take a field trip to Washington.<br><br>Learn about presidents of other countries and compare them to ours.<br><br>Write the president a letter.<br><br>Talk to someone who worked for a president. | **6. Give a few reasons why it is important to learn about this topic.**<br><br>Because the president can draft us to fight in a war.<br><br>Because we elect the president to make the right decision for us.<br><br>Because the president can make laws that help people get jobs.<br><br>The president decides how our taxes will be spent.<br><br>Because it helps you understand when people talk about it on the news. |

**Figure 1.6.** Eighth-grade students' responses to a Starting Block game about the U.S. presidency.

## Topic: Shakespeare's *Julius Caesar*

| | |
|---|---|
| **1. As a whole group, list as many questions as possible about this topic. Time limit: 3 minutes.**<br><br>How accurate is Shakespeare's account of Julius Caesar's death? / How long did it take him to write it? / What did the critics think of his play back then? / Why do we have to read this when we already studied it in Western Civ. class? / Did Shakespeare have to censor the stabbing scene? / Who is the real villain in this play? Cicero, Brutus, Antony? / Did people really talk like that in Shakespeare's time? / How could Shakespeare have researched the story before writing it? | **2. Invent two difficult questions about this topic. Ask the player on your right for help.**<br><br>How did the Roman people really react to Caesar's death? Did they know he was conspired against?<br><br>How would Shakespeare write the play if he were alive today? |
| **3. What might be the most interesting thing to learn about this topic? What might be the most boring?**<br><br>The most interesting thing to learn would be how we could do the play ourselves. The most boring would be stuff about Shakespeare's life.<br><br>Interesting: How Romans fought in wars in Caesar's time. Boring: Memorizing passages from the play.<br><br>It would be interesting to learn about what Roman life was like during Caesar's rule. The most boring thing would be all the new vocabulary words we'd have to study for a quiz. | **4. Each player in the group must list one thing they already know about this topic.**<br><br>Julius Caesar was emperor of Rome.<br><br>Caesar was stabbed by members of the Roman Senate.<br><br>He said, "Et tu, Brute!" when Brutus stabbed him.<br><br>Caesar died in 44 BC.<br><br>Shakespeare's supposed to be one of the greatest writers in the world (but I don't agree). |
| **5. What interesting steps could you take to learn more about this topic? List at least three ideas.**<br><br>Get some Cliff Notes.<br><br>Read the story again.<br><br>Talk to an actor who has played Caesar.<br><br>Ask the history teacher for books on Caesar and compare them to Shakespeare's version.<br><br>Go see the play performed somewhere. | **6. Give a few reasons why it is important to learn about this topic.**<br><br>It teaches you some history.<br><br>Because you learn what phrases like, "Beware the Ides of March" mean when you hear them.<br><br>One reason is people will think you're smart if you understand Shakespeare as it is written.<br><br>Because so many plays are based on the same themes Shakespeare used. |

**Figure 1.7.** Twelfth-grade students' responses to a Starting Block game about Shakespeare's *Julius Caesar*.

## Asking Thoughtful Questions

Identify and commend questions that...

go beyond the obvious, ask for explanations, make connections, show an unusual point of view or perspective, challenge assumptions, seem inventive or imaginative, ask for proof or justification, ask for clarification, pose problems, identify puzzles or mysteries.

**Examples**

*If the sun gives off so much light, why is it dark in space?*

*Where did the solar system come from?*

*How would civilization be different if we didn't know anything about the solar system?*

## Making Connections to Prior Knowledge

Identify and commend things students say they already know that...

make connections across subject matters, demonstrate logical connections (if... then...), make analogies, make predictions, are unusual or hard-to-remember facts.

**Examples**

*How is the presidency of the United States different from a king in a monarchy?*

*If the president can only be elected for two terms, then why can people in Congress get elected over and over?*

*What will the presidency be like 100 years from now?*

## Identifying Relevance

Identify and commend reasons students give for studying a topic that...

show thoughtfulness, demonstrate an inquisitive spirit, make connections across subject matters, make connections outside of school, are unusual or not obvious, show an appreciation of complexity.

**Examples**

*I wonder what kind of plays Shakespeare would be writing if he lived in one of our U.S. inner-city slums?*

*We talked about Caesar in Western Civ. class too, so how do we know which version is accurate according to history?*

*What would happen if students in Shakespeare's time had to read a playwright of ours like Arthur Miller. I wonder if they'd have as much trouble understanding him as we do Shakespeare?*

### Inventing Learning Strategies

Identify and commend steps students suggest for learning about a topic that...

> are unusual or inventive, show an appreciation for alternative sources of information, are self-directed, involve active learning, identify real-world experts.

> **Examples**

> *Find out who uses a lot of geometry for their jobs and have them come in and teach us.*

> *We could take a trip to the Fine Arts and Science Museums and compare how geometry was used on the stuff we saw in both places.*

> *We could try to teach it to someone and keep track of all the things we didn't explain too well.*

As you think about how to give feedback, keep in mind the power of language to communicate information. You can make your feedback informative by using the language associated with each category to identify students' thinking and commend it. For example, instead of simply saying "good idea" to a student, provide the student with more information about critical thinking by saying something like: "That's a thoughtful question because you are asking for evidence."

## *Where to Go from Here: Planning Future Lessons*

After students have played the Starting Block game, you may want to incorporate some of their ideas into upcoming lessons. After all, what better way to motivate students than to let their learning be guided by questions and ideas they themselves generate? Following are three ways to follow up on the Starting Block, followed by two sample scenarios that show how the results of the game might be used in future lessons. Though the scenarios don't offer step-by-step instruction, they may give you a sense of the kind of follow-up lessons that are appropriate for your students.

- Have students do a project based on a question or idea they generated while using the Starting Block. For example, while using the Starting Block in art class to explore Picasso, a student might wonder why Picasso distorts and rearranges the features of things he paints. As a project, the student might research abstract art and then revisit a recently completed artwork of his or her own to recast the piece as an abstract artist might.

- Use student-generated ideas to help redesign instruction. For example, you may decide to incorporate a focus on Japanese culture into a unit on World War II as a result of questions about Japan that emerged as students used the Starting Block.

- Use the questions generated while playing the Starting Block game to encourage students to reflect on what makes a good question and to develop criteria to use in formulating questions related to other subjects and topics.

## Independent Writing Projects

About halfway through a unit on World War I, Mr. Price used the Starting Block with his class of high school juniors. One reason Mr. Price decided to use the Starting Block midway through the unit was to boost students' energy level. But he had another purpose in mind, too. He wanted to help students think creatively about topics for an upcoming independent writing project that would culminate the unit. Over the next few weeks, each student was required to choose one aspect of World War I and write a report about it. Mr. Price guessed that the Starting Block would help students identify provocative, worthwhile research questions about the war and its era.

Students played the Starting Block game in small groups of four. As Mr. Price hoped, the groups were lively and spirited. Students were surprised by how much they already knew about World War I and also by how many questions they still had.

As students filed out the door at the end of class, one student lagged behind, stuffing notes and books into a knapsack.

"Mr. Price," she said, "I was just thinking about this writing project and the topics we decided to write about."

"Yes?"

"Well, one of the challenges I got when I rolled the Starting Block was the one about inventing a difficult question. So I asked whether World War I could teach us anything about where we are now as a country—the United States, I mean. Then I thought about what you said the other day, how England was a powerful country as far as the military goes when it fought World War I, but it wasn't really that strong because it was in so much debt to other countries before the war even started. That's one reason why the United States became a world leader after the war."

"Yes."

"Then I thought about the U.S. and all of our debt. Right now, we're the strongest in the world for war too, but is our debt so bad that another country is going to take our place as world leaders, like we did to England? It's weird. We seem to have a lot in common with them; we just finished a war, too. I was thinking of maybe doing a report that compared World War I England with the United States as it is now. Should I?"

Mr. Price smiled. Without glamour and fanfare, his student had made a high-level connection between the subject being studied and knowledge from contexts other than her U.S. history class. Of course, the proposal was ambitious, and the idea needed focus. Still, it was promising.

"Your idea has a lot of potential," Mr. Price said. "Why don't you jot down a few ideas about the connections you see, and come talk to me again after class tomorrow. If it still interests you, I believe we could shape your idea into a really exciting research project."

## Identifying Good Questions

Ms. King, a fifth-grade teacher, used the Starting Block in an introductory science lesson on electricity. Peering over students' shoulders as they worked, she was struck by the number of genuinely deep and provocative questions students asked. Knowing that asking good questions is important in all subjects, not just science, she decided to take the opportunity to encourage her students to reflect on what it is, exactly, that makes a question good.

After the groups finished playing the game, Ms. King asked each to group to choose two questions from their lists that they thought were the most difficult or thought-provoking.

Ms. King recorded the questions on the blackboard, then she told students to read over all of the questions on the board carefully. After a moment, she asked, "What makes these questions good? What are the signs that tell you these are good questions?"

After a moment, one student responded cautiously, "Questions that make you explain things?"

"Good idea," Ms. King said and started a new list with the heading Good Questions Are Questions that…. Underneath she wrote "…ask for explanations."

"What's another sign of a good question?" she asked.

"Good questions make you give reasons, not just yes-or-no answers," said another student.

"I can tell a good question when there's no definite answer to it; people have to debate it for a long time," a third student said.

Another student chimed in to say questions that start with the word *why* always make her think hard.

Ms. King recorded all the comments on the board. Eventually, she worked with students to group and combine the collected comments and to refine them into a short set of good-question criteria. She explained that good questions were important in all subject areas and that she hoped students would use these criteria to help them ask good questions in all the different topics they study.

"I'm going to make this list into a giant wall poster," she said. "I'll leave it up on the classroom wall, so we'll always be reminded of how to ask a good question. And I'll leave extra room on the poster, so if we think of more good-question criteria as the school year progresses, we can add them to the list."

# 2

# Whatzit
# Tic-Tac-Toe

## How Whatzit Tic-Tac-Toe Cultivates Critical Thinking and Understanding

How would you describe a microscope? Photosynthesis? Aztec civilization? Calculus? In a way, asking students to describe things is very much a part of traditional instruction: We ask students to describe such things as scientific concepts and procedures; important historical events; social customs; and key topics, themes, and ideas. It's easy to describe these sorts of things superficially, mentioning only their obvious characteristics (e.g., the physical parts of a microscope or the steps in the process of photosynthesis). But most things in the world have many different kinds of features—obvious and hidden, important and not-so-important—and developing a deep understanding of something involves probing beneath its obvious characteristics to build an elaborate mental model of its diverse features and how they are interrelated.

For example, consider the difference between asking students to describe the obvious features of a human hand—fingers, bones, fingernails, and so on—and asking them questions like: What are the important features of the human hand? Which features are less important, and why? What are some very different kinds of features? What's a hidden feature, a can't-do-without feature, a hard-to-understand feature? Whatzit Tic-Tac-Toe asks these sorts of questions. In doing so, it cultivates critical thinking and understanding in the following ways:

- **Looking for analogies.** Teachers have long appreciated the power of analogy. Sometimes the most interesting features of something are revealed by comparing it to something else. Whatzit Tic-Tac-Toe challenges students to deepen their understanding of what they are studying by constructing obvious as well as less obvious analogies.

- **Evaluating the relative importance of features.** Whatzit Tic-Tac-Toe asks students to go beyond surface descriptions to make judgments about which features of a thing are essential, important, and not so important.

- **Thinking creatively about different kinds of features.** Things have many kinds of features. Consider a smile. A smile has physical, observable features (teeth, lips); functional features (it can express joy or conceal sorrow); aesthetic features (there are pretty smiles, glamorous smiles), and so on. Whatzit Tic-Tac-Toe challenges students to think broadly and divergently about the different kinds of features things have.

## When to Use Whatzit Tic-Tac-Toe

**Use Whatzit Tic-Tac-Toe any time students have enough prior knowledge or enough new knowledge about a topic to be able to identify several of its features.**

The more students know about a topic, the easier it is to play Whatzit Tic-Tac-Toe. But students don't need to be experts to benefit from playing the game. Please don't wait until the end of a topic or unit to use the Whatzit game. The game boosts students' interest in a topic and provides a good foundation for further learning.

**Use Whatzit Tic-Tac-Toe immediately before using the Whyzit Cube on the same topic.**

Description and explanation are familiar, yet powerful, thinking moves students can make toward deeper understanding. Unfortunately, most students don't engage in or execute these key thinking moves enough. In general, Whatzit Tic-Tac-Toe challenges students to construct rich descriptions of topics or ideas, while the Whyzit Cube challenges students to reason about and explain those topics and ideas. Certainly, Whatzit Tic-Tac-Toe cultivates deeper understanding when played as a standalone activity. But when used together, Whatzit Tic-Tac-Toe and the Whyzit Cube provide students with a broader range of opportunities to think critically about a particular topic or idea.

If you decide to use Whatzit Tic-Tac-Toe and the Whyzit Cube in sequence, be sure to select a topic that is appropriate for both games. Many topics map easily over Whatzit Tic-Tac-Toe and the Whyzit Cube, but some do not. See pages 42–43 to help you determine whether the topic you have selected is appropriate for both games.

## Getting Started

1.  Choose a topic you would like students to understand better. A Whatzit can be an idea, concept, theme, theory, event, object, or process. For example, it can be a poem, the scientific method, a number line, multiplication, the electoral college, the knee joint, the voyage of Darwin's *Beagle,* the concept of civilization, or a computer.

    NOTE: Whatzit Tic-Tac-Toe and the Whyzit Cube (chapter 3) can be played sequentially with the same topic. If you plan to use both games, choose a topic that will work for both of them. *All* Whyzit Cube topics are suitable for Whatzit Tic-Tac-Toe—but some Whatzit topics *are not* suitable for use with the Whyzit Cube. For more information on topics that are suitable for the Whyzit Cube game, see chapter 3.

2.  Schedule a time for students to play Whatzit Tic-Tac-Toe. (See the When to Use Whatzit Tic-Tac-Toe section of this chapter for more suggestions about when to use the game.) Typically, a game takes 10–20 minutes to play. The game can be played any time students have enough prior knowledge or new information about a topic to think carefully about its features.

3.  Group students into pairs or teams of four. If students are in groups of four, have them play in teams of two against two. Give each group

    ■ a Whatzit Tic-Tac-Toe master game piece (figure 2.1)

    ■ a Response Sheet (figure 2.2)

4.  Explain the rules and review the definitions aloud. Either post the rules and definitions where students can easily refer to them, or give each group a copy. (See figure 2.3 for rules.)

    Remind students that the object of Whatzit Tic-Tac-Toe is not simply to win the game. A more important objective is to think deeply about the thinking challenges at hand, and produce responses that are reasonable, plausible, or creative. Players should *not* challenge a player's or team's response simply to prevent them from winning!

    Players should challenge responses from another player or team only if they sense that a response is *absolutely* implausible or unreasonable. Chances are, if players are serious about their thinking, their responses will be more than acceptable and highly resistant to challenge.

5. Remind groups to record their responses on the Response Sheet. Collect the sheets when students are done. If you wish, provide written or verbal feedback using the Guidelines for Feedback in this chapter.

6. See the Where to Go from Here section of this chapter for suggestions about how to connect students' work to future lessons.

# The Whatzit is:

| | | |
|---|---|---|
| List three important features of the Whatzit. | List three not-so-important (trivial or superficial) features of the Whatzit. | List two very different *kinds* of features of the Whatzit. |
| Identify a hidden feature of the Whatzit—a feature most people wouldn't notice or think of. | What is one feature without which the Whatzit would be entirely different? | Which feature of the Whatzit is hardest to understand? Why? |
| Which of the Whatzit's features do you find most interesting? Why? | Think of something you know about that is very different from the Whatzit. List two ways it is different and one way it is similar. | Think of something you know about that is very similar to the Whatzit. List two ways it is similar and one way it is different. |

**Figure 2.1.** Whatzit Tic-Tac-Toe master game sheet.

# Whatzit Tic-Tac-Toe Response Sheet

The Whatzit is: _____

Names: _____

_____

**Challenge 1**

List three important features of the Whatzit.

**Challenge 2**

List three not-so-important (trivial or superficial) features of the Whatzit.

**Figure 2.2.** Whatzit Tic-Tac-Toe Response Sheet.

## Whatzit Tic-Tac-Toe Response Sheet (continued)

### Challenge 3
List two very different *kinds* of features of the Whatzit.

### Challenge 4
Identify a hidden feature of the Whatzit—a feature most people wouldn't notice or think of.

### Challenge 5
What is one feature without which the Whatzit would be entirely different?

**Figure 2.2** Whatzit Tic-Tac-Toe Response Sheet (continued).

## Whatzit Tic-Tac-Toe Response Sheet (continued)

**Challenge 6**
Which feature of the Whatzit is the hardest to understand? Why?

**Challenge 7**
Which of the Whatzit's features do you find the most interesting? Why?

**Figure 2.2.** Whatzit Tic-Tac-Toe Response Sheet (continued).

## Whatzit Tic-Tac-Toe Response Sheet (continued)

**Challenge 8**

Think of something you know about that is very different from the Whatzit. List two ways it is different and one way it is similar.

**Challenge 9**

Think of something you know about that is very similar to the Whatzit. List two ways it is similar and one way it is different.

**Figure 2.2.** Whatzit Tic-Tac-Toe Response Sheet (continued).

# *Rules of Whatzit Tic-Tac-Toe*

*For two players or two teams of players.*

1. Each player or team tries to fill three squares in a row (horizontal, vertical, or diagonal). The first team or player to get three answers in a row wins the game.

2. To fill a square, the player or team must fully answer the question in the corresponding square on the master game sheet.

3. All answers must be written on the Response Sheet.

4. Before writing an answer on the Response Sheet, all players on both teams must agree that the answer is acceptable. If full agreement can't be reached, all players must vote. If there are only two players and they disagree about the acceptability of an answer, or if the vote among the teams is a tie, an outside person must be asked to decide. If an answer is judged to be unacceptable, the team or player may try to answer the question one more time.

   If the second response a team makes is also judged unacceptable, the team loses its turn and the square remains blank.

**Figure 2.3.** Rules and definitions for Whatzit Tic-Tac-Toe.

From *Critical Squares: Games of Critical Thinking and Understanding.* © 1997.
Teacher Ideas Press 1-800-237-6124.

The object of Whatzit Tic-Tac-Toe is not simply to win the game, but to think deeply about the topic. Do *not* challenge a player's or a team's response simply to prevent them from winning! Instead, challenge a response only when you believe that it is *absolutely* unreasonable. Creative or unusual responses can be good; think twice before you challenge!

## Definitions

### Whatzit

An object, idea, event, concept, theory, or process—that is, anything at all! Examples: a pencil, multiplication, the number line, the concept of justice, creation myths, punctuation, haiku, baseball, friendship, families, a microscope, a smile, photosynthesis, the Pythagorean theorem.

### Feature

A physical or nonphysical attribute or dimension of the Whatzit topic. Generally, physical features are those you can determine by looking at, or examining, a topic. For example, lead is a physical feature of a pencil. Its size and shape are other physical features. An example of a nonphysical feature of a pencil would be its breakability.

**Figure 2.3.** Rules and definitions for Whatzit Tic-Tac-Toe (continued).

From *Critical Squares: Games of Critical Thinking and Understanding.* © 1997.
Teacher Ideas Press 1-800-237-6124.

## Sample Student Responses

Describing something fully is more difficult than it seems. Often our descriptions merely dance on the surface of the ideas or objects like starlight on shimmering water. Whatzit Tic-Tac-Toe encourages students to examine the important and sometimes intriguing features of ideas or objects that lie beneath the surface of things and to ponder how those features relate to each other.

Just as describing something can be deceptively simple, students find Whatzit Tic-Tac-Toe accessible and challenging. Several students have enjoyed the game even though it was harder than they expected. "I never thought there was so much to learn from making a good description," said one eighth grader.

Figures 2.4–2.7 provide examples of responses from students in actual classroom settings. Take a moment or two to review these examples to get a sense of the kinds of responses you can expect the first time you play Whatzit Tic-Tac-Toe in your classroom.

## Guidelines for Feedback: Responding to Students' Thinking

The questions and comments we respond to, and how we respond to them, send clear messages to students about the types of thinking we recognize and value. That's why it's important to provide balanced and informative feedback that clearly communicates to students information about their own thinking and learning processes. As students play Whatzit Tic-Tac-Toe, identify and commend responses or questions that

- Identify analogies or make comparisons

- Evaluate the relative importance of features

- Indicate creative thinking about various features

When students make comments that fall into one of the categories listed above, it indicates that they are thinking critically about the topic. Following are some aspects of critical thinking to look for in each category, along with examples drawn from actual student responses.

### Looking for Analogies, Making Comparisons

Identify and commend responses that...

make comparisons to various features or to other topics, make connections to something students know about, reveal some interesting or hidden dimension of the feature or topic, recognize obvious and not-so-obvious similarities and differences of features.

**Examples**

*Rock is different from a scientist in that a rock is not alive; but it is similar because some rocks have colors similar to shades of skin.*

*Calculus is similar to engineering in that engineering is complex and has a lot of formulas too. It's different because you use calculus to do engineering, not the other way around.*

*The Mayans are similar to the Aztecs in that they had similar foods and built similar temples; they are different because Mayans didn't perform human sacrifices.*

## Evaluating the Relative Importance of Features

Identify and commend responses that...

rank the importance of certain features, reconfigure features or designs, point out strengths or weaknesses of features, recognize the relevance of specific features to the topic in general.

### Examples

*The Spanish conquerors were an important feature for Aztec civilization. Without them, the Aztecs might still be around.*

*Being able to write is an important feature for scientists. Without it, they couldn't record their findings.*

*An important feature of calculus is that it can measure the area of weird shapes and surfaces.*

## Thinking Creatively About Different Features

Identify and commend responses that...

reveal some aspect or dimension that is surprising or original; indicate possible hidden or alternative uses, dimensions, or outcomes; force you to look or think about the topic in a new way; show a divergent perspective or focus.

### Examples

*A human heart is the same as the Aztec Civilization because both need to be alive to function right.*

*Scientists are curious and creative without knowing what's going to happen next.*

*Categories are important, because if there were none, we'd have to describe everything by color, size, and shape, instead of just one name.*

# The Whatzit is: Scientists

| | | |
|---|---|---|
| **List three important features of the Whatzit.**<br><br>Always experimenting.<br><br>Always seem to work alone.<br><br>Has microscope and science tools around. | **List three not-so-important features of the Whatzit.**<br><br>Wears glasses or not.<br><br>What they look like.<br><br>How tall they are. | **List two very different *kinds* of features of the Whatzit.**<br><br>Has to take good notes.<br><br>Has to know a lot of math. |
| **Identify a hidden feature of the Whatzit—a feature most people wouldn't notice or think of.**<br><br>They have to do a lot of research and studying. | **What is one feature without which the Whatzit would be entirely different?**<br><br>Writing: If they couldn't write, they coudn't record their discoveries. | **Which feature of the Whatzit is hardest to understand? Why?**<br><br>Why they wear white coats. It looks like doctors' clothes. |
| **Which of the Whatzit's features do you find most interesting? Why?**<br><br>They are creative and curious without knowing what's going to happen next, like George Washington Carver. | **Think of something you know about that is very different from the Whatzit. List two ways it is different and one way it is similar.**<br><br>A rock: It's different because it isn't alive and it can't get hurt. It's similar because some rocks have the same color as skin. | **Think of something you know about that is very similar to the Whatzit. List two ways it is similar and one way it is different.**<br><br>Math: It's the same because you have to experiment and you have to be a good reader. It's different because math has more rules. |

**Figure 2.4.** Fifth-grade students' responses to a Whatzit Tic-Tac-Toe game about scientists.

# The Whatzit is: Classification

| List three important features of the Whatzit. | List three not-so-important features of the Whatzit. | List two very different *kinds* of features of the Whatzit. |
|---|---|---|
| The categories of species: monerans, protists, and animals.<br><br>It gives us a way to organize things into groups.<br><br>Have to look closely at things to tell which group they belong to. | There are 10 million animals; only 2 million have been classified.<br><br>One animal species is discovered a week.<br><br>Coral lives underwater, but it can't drown. | Autotrophs can make their own food, while echinoderms need to hunt or go out to get their food. |
| **Identify a hidden feature of the Whatzit—a feature most people wouldn't notice or think of.**<br><br>Many cnidarians are symmetrical in some way. If you cut them in half, both halves are the same. | **What is one feature without which the Whatzit would be entirely different?**<br><br>Categories. If there were none, we'd have to describe everything by color, size, and shape, instead of just giving it one general name. | **Which feature of the Whatzit is hardest to understand? Why?**<br><br>Why coral has plant life on it. It doesn't look alive, but it is living and supports other living things. |
| **Which of the Whatzit's features do you find most interesting? Why?**<br><br>The cnidarians are unique because no other animals can do what they do. | **Think of something you know about that is very different from the Whatzit. List two ways it is different and one way it is similar.**<br><br>A book: Different because it is not a living thing, and it doesn't evolve. Same because the author is a living thing and had to evolve to write it. | **Think of something you know about that is very similar to the Whatzit. List two ways it is similar and one way it is different.**<br><br>A computer. Same because you have to arrange files into categories and they are always changing. Different because a computer isn't living. |

**Figure 2.5.** Eighth-grade students' responses to a Whatzit Tic-Tac-Toe game about classification.

# The Whatzit is: Aztec civilization

| **List three important features of the Whatzit.** | **List three not-so-important features of the Whatzit.** | **List two very different *kinds* of features of the Whatzit.** |
|---|---|---|
| They had advanced technology (tools, buildings, writing).<br><br>They were arranged in communities.<br><br>They had their own language. | They blew their nose into their hands.<br><br>300,000 people living in the main city.<br><br>Main city is where Mexico City is now. | The Aztecs were so advanced in astronomy, space, calendar making, and science, but they believed in human sacrifice. |
| **Identify a hidden feature of the Whatzit—a feature most people wouldn't notice or think of.**<br><br>A hidden feature is that they were very civilized, even though they don't seem it from looking at them. | **What is one feature without which the Whatzit would be entirely different?**<br><br>One feature could be the Spanish conquerors. If they didn't show up, there still might be Aztecs. | **Which feature of the Whatzit is hardest to understand? Why?**<br><br>The Aztecs were warlike. But I don't understand why they didn't fight with the Mayans who lived close by. |
| **Which of the Whatzit's features do you find most interesting? Why?**<br><br>The monuments and the pyramids they built. It's tough to imagine how they built those things way back then. | **Think of something you know about that is very different from the Whatzit. List two ways it is different and one way it is similar.**<br><br>A human heart: It's different because you can see a heart, and it is living flesh. It's the same because both need to be alive to work right. | **Think of something you know about that is very similar to the Whatzit. List two ways it is similar and one way it is different.**<br><br>Mayans: Mayans are similar because of their foods and they built similar temples and buildings. Different because Mayans did not do human sacrifices. |

**Figure 2.6.** Eighth-grade students' responses to a Whatzit Tic-Tac-Toe game about Aztec civilization.

# The Whatzit is: Calculus

| **List three important features of the Whatzit.** | **List three not-so-important features of the Whatzit.** | **List two very different *kinds* of features of the Whatzit.** |
| --- | --- | --- |
| Deals with numbers and formulas.<br><br>The concepts of integrals, derivatives, and exponents.<br><br>It measures area and volume of weird shapes surfaces. | Applying it to regular geometry, like right triangles.<br><br>Calculators and textbooks.<br><br>History of calculus. We just need to know how to do it. | One feature is that you need to understand Algebra II before you understand calculus; another is that you can do a lot of calculus on a calculator. People understand things, calculators don't. |
| **Identify a hidden feature of the Whatzit—a feature most people wouldn't notice or think of.** | **What is one feature without which the Whatzit would be entirely different?** | **Which feature of the Whatzit is hardest to understand? Why?** |
| Calculus can be used to solve problems you wouldn't think of, like doing landscape work, surveying, figuring azimuths for navigation. | One feature is that it works. If it couldn't be used to solve real problems in the world, it would be just another theory and wouldn't get taught in schools. | The idea of limits, because it is all so vague at first until you can visualize it in your head. |
| **Which of the Whatzit's features do you find most interesting? Why?** | **Think of something you know about that is very different from the Whatzit. List two ways it is different and one way it is similar.** | **Think of something you know about that is very similar to the Whatzit. List two ways it is similar and one way it is different.** |
| Reducing equations is interesting because it breaks the big problem into manageable pieces. | History class: It's different because history deals with the past and more facts. It's the same because we learn it in school. | Engineering: It's similar because engineering is complex and has a lot of formulas. It's different because you use calculus to do engineering, not the other way around. |

**Figure 2.7.** Twelfth-grade students' responses to a Whatzit Tic-Tac-Toe game about calculus.

# Where to Go from Here: Planning Future Lessons

One easy yet powerful way to supplement Whatzit Tic-Tac-Toe is to play the Whyzit Cube game. When played in sequence, the games take advantage of students' basic familiarity with generating descriptions and explanations by bringing both of those thinking enterprises to bear on a particular topic or idea. But relying on a Whatzit/Whyzit combination is far from your only option.

You'll find that thoughtful descriptions are like captivating paintings or photographs—they draw you in and demand inspection and inquiry. As you let yourself be drawn into the descriptions students make using Whatzit Tic-Tac-Toe, ask yourself the following questions:

- What kinds of analogies did students make? What might the analogies suggest about how well students understand the topic? What's accurate or fresh about their analogies? What's faulty about them?

- What kinds of features or dimensions did students tend to identify most? Did they discuss important features, or did they hover over unimportant or trivial features?

- What new ideas or perspectives did you notice in students' responses? What might these new perspectives suggest about students' interest in and understanding of the topic?

The following sample scenarios illustrate how a teacher could follow up on Whatzit Tic-Tac-Toe. Though the scenarios don't offer step-by-step instructions, they may give you a sense of the kind of follow-up lessons that are possible.

## Enriching Descriptions for Deeper Understanding

Ms. Makita used Whatzit Tic-Tac-Toe with her fifth-grade class after a morning field trip to the local science museum. Immediately following the visit to the museum, she gave students this task: In pairs, identify an object or idea from one of the exhibits they found interesting. Then, play Whatzit Tic-Tac-Toe using the object or idea as the Whatzit.

Some students chose exhibits related to subjects they had studied in class; others explored exhibits that were unrelated to the curriculum. Later that evening, as Ms. Makita reviewed students' responses, she noticed that although students generated highly detailed descriptions of the exhibits, she could not tell whether her students understood the difference between the trivial and important features. Wanting to find out what students perceive as important and not-so-important features, she designed a follow-up lesson that asked students to revisit their responses to the first two Whatzit challenges:

- List three important features of the Whatzit.

- List three not-so-important features of the Whatzit.

She asked the students to choose any three of their responses to those challenges and explain on paper what was important or not-so-important about the features they identified. Ms. Makita figured that by asking students to do this evaluative reasoning, she'd have enough information to help her develop other lessons that might encourage students to use description more effectively to build understanding.

## Making Connections: Comparing Art Forms

Mr. Brooks, a high school English teacher, used Whatzit Tic-Tac-Toe after he and his class saw *The Adventures of Huckleberry Finn* performed by a professional theater company. Instead of discussing the play as a class, Mr. Brooks asked his students to play the Whatzit game to help them uncover some hidden features of the play and possibly to encourage students' to connect features of the performance to the book, which they had only just started to read.

Mr. Brooks collected their responses and decided to look them over later on that day. When he did, he noticed students did not do a very good job of finding meaningful similarities or differences between the play and other topics. One student wrote, "A book is similar because it tells a story, and it's different because there no real actors." Another wrote, "A movie is similar to a play because you have to go a theater to see it, and it's different because the play is more expensive." As he continued to review their responses, he noticed other instances of students making superficial observations. Mr. Brooks was hoping that the analogy challenges in the Whatzit game would help students develop a deeper understanding of the play's important themes and characterizations. Mr. Brooks decided to try to explicitly encourage students to make deeper comparisons to other topics and ideas.

The next day in class, Mr. Brooks handed back the response sheets from the day before and asked the students to review their responses to questions the analogy challenges:

Think of something you know about that is very different from the Whatzit. List two ways it is different and one way it is similar.

Think of something you know that is very similar to the Whatzit. List two ways it is similar and one way it is different.

Mr. Brooks asked students to list more similarities and differences between the theater production and the book. But this time he urged students to seek unusual, creative, or hidden comparisons. He also urged students to go beneath the surface and look for deep and important connections. Then he handed each student a blank sheet of paper and asked them to write their new responses to the challenges. While students worked, Mr. Brooks noticed some immediate improvement in their responses. One student noted that the novel was similar to the play because "both can have a moral for people to learn from." Another student wrote, "The book was different from the play in that the book makes you use your imagination, where the play lets you sit back and just watch." Mr. Brooks found these responses encouraging.

# The Whyzit
# Cube Game

## How the Whyzit Cube Cultivates Critical Thinking and Understanding

The question Why? is probably the most frequently asked question under the sun. And as any teacher knows, Why? can mean several different things. For instance, sometimes why-questions ask for an explanation, such as, Why is the sky blue? Other times they ask for a rationale or justification, such as, Why do we have to go to school? or Why is there space exploration?

This second type of why-question is the focus of the Whyzit Cube. The Whyzit Cube helps students explore the purposes of things. In the process, it invites them to think about how well a thing's purposes are met and how a thing could be improved to meet its purposes even better.

Most things conceived of or designed by humans have purposes, and exploring their purposes can be quite a challenge, especially when we've come to take them for granted. For example, consider the challenge of questions like What is the purpose of a city? What's the purpose of space exploration? Of public education? Of the concept of democracy? Of a novel? Of the scientific method? Of the study of anthropology? Of team sports? Using the Whyzit Cube cultivates critical thinking and understanding because it engages students in analyzing and evaluating the deep structure of these sorts of things—why they're made the way they are, what they're supposed to do, and how well they work.

Specifically, the Whyzit Cube builds critical thinking and understanding in the following ways:

- **Identifying key and unusual purposes.** Most things have key purposes as well as unusual purposes. For example, a key purpose of a house is to provide shelter. But there are other, less apparent, purposes that houses serve, too. A house might also serve as a gathering place for friends or family. Another purpose of a house is that it can serve as a source of income or equity for those who own one. The Whyzit Cube pushes students to go beyond the obvious to identify a variety of purposes, including unusual or hidden purposes.

- **Identifying applications and examples.** Part of understanding how something works is being able to recognize what it looks like in practice. For example, understanding the concept of democracy means being able to recognize opportunities to apply democratic principles and also being able to recognize situations in which democratic principles are absent.

- **Evaluating how well something works.** Critical thinking involves being able to evaluate the effectiveness of things—how well they achieve their purposes and where they fall short. For example, thinking critically about space exploration involves examining the ways in which it achieves its purposes and the ways in which it doesn't.

- **Thinking creatively about improvements.** With a little creativity, it's possible to imagine improvements on just about anything. The Whyzit Cube challenges students' creativity by asking them to imagine ways to make taken-for-granted objects and ideas more interesting and more effective.

## When to Use the Whyzit Cube

**Use the Whyzit Cube any time students know enough about something to be able to think about what it is used for and how well it works.**

You don't have to know everything about a topic in order to think about its purposes. Consider a house. Students may not know everything there is to know about houses, but they certainly know enough to think about the purposes of a house—what it is for and how well it works. Use the Whyzit Cube in the middle of a topic or unit, when students have enough content knowledge to be able to probe a Whyzit's purposes, even if they're not yet experts.

**Use the Whyzit Cube to follow up Whatzit Tic-Tac-Toe.**

The Whatzit and Whyzit games are designed to be used sequentially, because describing the features of something is only half its story. Truly understanding an object, concept, or event also involves understanding what its features are for. Use these games together when you have a topic that invites deep understanding.

## Getting Started

1. Choose a Whyzit topic you would like students to understand better. A Whyzit can be anything except a force of nature or a natural phenomenon. Sometimes teachers like to play the Whyzit game with the same topic they used for Whatzit Tic-Tac-Toe.

   NOTE: Topics that work for the Whyzit Cube are limited to those that are either designed to serve a particular purpose or are made by humans. Topics that aren't well suited for use with the Whyzit Cube are forces of nature or natural phenomena like trees, tornadoes, rocks, clouds, or lions. Figure 3.1 includes a definition of a Whyzit topic and offers a partial list of topics for this game.

2. Schedule a time for students to play the Whyzit Cube game. The game may be played any time students have enough prior knowledge or new information about a topic to think carefully about its purposes. Typically, a game takes 10–20 minutes to play. (See the When to Use the Whyzit Cube section of this chapter for more suggestions about when to use the Whyzit Cube.)

3. Have students work in small groups, with 3–5 students in each group. Give each group

   - a Whyzit Cube game piece, pre-assembled or to assemble themselves (pattern appears in figure 3.2)
   - a Response Sheet (figure 3.3)

4. Explain the rules and the definition of a Whyzit aloud, and either post the rules and definition where students can easily refer to them, or give each group a copy of the rules. (See figure 3.4 for rules and definition.)

5. Remind groups to record their responses on the Response Sheet as they play the game. Collect the sheets when the groups are done. If you wish, provide written or verbal feedback using the Guidelines for Feedback in this chapter.

6. See the Where to Go from Here section of this chapter for suggestions about how to build on the Whyzit Cube in future lessons.

# What Is a Whyzit?

A Whyzit is an object, idea, event, concept, theory, or process that is neither a force of nature nor a natural phenomenon.

## Sample Topics That Will Work with the Whyzit Cube.

**Language Arts and Literature**
a diary
a conductor
a novel
a comic book
a card catalog

**Social Studies**
an army
congress
a flag
the president
communities
monarchy

**Math**
a computer
zero
a number line
an abacus
calculus
multiplication
a calculator
the Pythagorean
  theorem

**Science**
the heart
a microscope
the Periodic Table
a scientist
vitamins

**Music**
musical theatre
a conductor
an orchestra
scales
a cello

**General**
fairness
homework
a bicycle
civilization
jails
laws
families
a home
a museum

**Art**
a crayon
an artist
finger paint
a mosaic
sculpture
architecture
ballet

**Physical Education**
team sports
team spirit
an athelete
competition
sportmanship

NOTE: All Whyzit topics will also work with Whatzit Tic-Tac-Toe.

**Figure 3.1.** Definition and sample topics for the Whyzit Cube.

**1.**

What are the main purposes of the Whyzit? What are the most important things it is supposed to do or be used for?

**2.**

What is an unusual purpose of the Whyzit? How could the Whyzit be applied or used in an unusual way?

**3.**

When would it be wrong to use the Whyzit? When would it be misapplied or out of place? Explain.

**4.**

All players: Brainstorm at least four ways to change the Whyzit to make it better, more interesting, or more effective. Be imaginative!

**5.**

How well does the Whyzit work? List two reasons why the Whyzit works well and two reasons why the Whyzit might need improvement. Ask the player on your left for help.

**6.**

Identify two examples of the Whyzit in action. Think of situations, instances, or places where people use or apply the Whyzit.

*To assemble: Cut along the solid lines, fold on the dotted lines, and tape together to form a cube.*

**Figure 3.2.** The Whyzit Cube game piece.

# Whyzit Cube Response Sheet

Topic: _____

Names: _____

_____

Record your responses for each roll of the Whyzit Cube. If the same challenge is rolled twice, just add the responses to the correct column.

## Challenge 1
What are the main purposes of the Whyzit? What are the most important things it is supposed to do or be used for?

## Challenge 2
What is an unusual purpose of the Whyzit? How could the Whyzit be applied or used in an unusual way?

**Figure 3.3.** Whyzit Cube Response Sheet.

## Whyzit Cube Response Sheet (continued)

**Challenge 3**

When would it be wrong to use the Whyzit? When would it be misapplied or out of place? Explain.

**Challenge 4**

All players: Brainstorm at least four ways to change the Whyzit to make it better, more interesting, or more effective. Be imaginative!

**Figure 3.3.** Whyzit Cube Response Sheet (continued).

## Whyzit Cube Response Sheet (continued)

**Challenge 5**

How well does the Whyzit work? List two reasons why the Whyzit works well and two reasons why the Whyzit might need improvement. Ask the player on your left for help.

**Challenge 6**

Identify two examples of the Whyzit in action. Think of situations, instances, or places where people use or apply the Whyzit.

**Figure 3.3.** Whyzit Cube Response Sheet (continued).

# *Rules of the Whyzit Cube Game*

*For groups of 3–5 players.*

1. Players take turns rolling the die. Each player has one roll per turn. The player with the last birthday in the calendar year rolls first.

2. Roll the die and answer the thinking challenge that faces up. The player who rolls the die records his or her responses on the Whyzit Cube Response Sheet.

3. Go around the circle twice, so each player has two turns.

4. Some questions ask the whole group to respond. For group challenges, the player who rolls the die records the group's responses on the Response Sheet.

5. Sometimes, the same thinking challenge comes up two times in a row. If this happens, the player or group must respond to the challenge again. If the challenge comes up more than two times in a row, roll the die again for a new thinking challenge.

**Figure 3.4.** Rules and definition for the Whyzit Cube game.

# *Definition*

## Whyzit

An object, idea, event, concept, theory, or process that is neither a force of nature nor a natural phenomenon. Whyzit topics include a computer, the concept of civilization, an army, a holiday, geometry, musical notation, museums, *The Iliad,* long division, breakfast cereals, baseball, friendship, families, computer animation, advertising. Whyzits *are not* natural phenomena like thunderstorms, earthquakes, trees, rain, mountains, mammals, stars, or planets.

**Figure 3.4.** Rules and definition for the Whyzit Cube game (continued).

## Sample Student Responses

A sound explanation is multidimensional. Justifying, rationalizing, exploring the purposes and effectiveness of things can all be considered types of explanation. The Whyzit Cube challenges students to generate several different kinds of explanations around a single topic or idea to help ensure understanding.

Figures 3.5–3.8 provide responses students generated while playing the Whyzit Cube in their regular classrooms. Although many of the students' responses are exemplary, it is important to remember that these are real examples, not idealized ones. Some responses are stronger than others. The reason we have included authentic rather than ideal examples here and throughout the book is to give you a better idea of what to expect in your own classroom.

## Guidelines for Feedback: Responding to Students' Thinking

As you review figures 3.5–3.8, you will notice that some responses are better than others. Some responses address the thinking challenges directly and creatively; others, though sometimes interesting or provocative, missed the point. Though we discourage you from grading students' responses, we encourage you to offer appropriate feedback to help students gauge how well they are doing and how critically they are thinking about the topic. As students play the Whyzit Cube game, look for responses or ideas that:

- Seek key and unusual purposes

- Seek applications and examples

- Evaluate how well something works

Following are some things to look for under each category, along with some examples from actual student responses.

### Seek Key and Unusual Purposes

Identify and commend responses that...

uncover hidden purposes; indicate multiple or alternative purposes; speculate on design, structure, or organization; indicate an understanding of central or important purposes or ideas.

#### Examples

*A key purpose of a novel is to gather information about a person or about the past.*

*An unusual or hidden purpose of baseball is to teach cooperation and team spirit.*

*A key purpose of a civilization is to bring people together into communities.*

## Seek Applications and Examples

Identify and commend responses that...

illustrate examples of the topic being used or in practice; recognize obvious and not-so-obvious opportunities to apply the topic; identify instances when the topic is misapplied or misused.

### Examples

*It might not be good to use animation to talk about serious topics like drugs or politics.*

*Civilization applies to the United States because we have lots of resources and lots of people, so we need to be civilized about it.*

*Novels could be used in language arts class to teach about different kinds of people.*

## Evaluate How Well Something Works

Identify and commend responses that...

assess or examine the effectiveness of the topic in practice, suggest areas for improvement, highlight areas of weakness, comment on how well the topic achieves its purpose.

### Examples

*Civilizations work well because there is less death and crime in a civilization, but there is still unemployment and overpopulation in many civilizations.*

*Animation would be more effective if it was more realistic without looking artificial or computerized.*

*Baseball works well because it does help you have fun and meet friends, but it's too slow sometimes, and there aren't many penalties for poor sportsmanship.*

## Topic: Novels

| | |
|---|---|
| **1. What are the main purposes of the Whyzit? What are the most important things it is supposed to do or be used for?**<br><br>People use novels to gather information. Like biographical novels to learn about a person, or historical fiction to learn about the past. | **2. What is an unusual purpose of the Whyzit? How could the Whyzit be applied or used in an unusual way?**<br><br>To read one just for the fun of it. Most of the time, we have to read them in school. Maybe we could use it instead of a textbook? |
| **3. When would it be wrong to use the Whyzit? When would it be misapplied or out of place? Explain.**<br><br>When you like a book so much you read it instead of doing something else, like math or science. It would be out of place in a restaurant, because you're supposed to eat, not read. | **4. All players: Brainstorm at least four ways to change the Whyzit to make it better, more interesting, or more effective. Be imaginative!**<br><br>Novels should have more sequels, so the story can go on.<br><br>Novels should have less quotations, they just slow things down.<br><br>Titles should be more interesting to make you want to read it.<br><br>It'd be better if we could read them on the computer. |
| **5. How well does the Whyzit work? List two reasons why the Whyzit works well and two reasons why the Whyzit might need improvement. Ask the player on your left for help.**<br><br>Works well: A good novel can get you interested in a topic by giving lots of details about it you don't get from workbooks.<br><br>Needs improvement: Some novels have bad language that isn't necessary to the story. | **6. Identify two examples of the Whyzit in action. Think of situations, instances, or places where people use or apply the Whyzit.**<br><br>In language arts class to teach about different kinds of people.<br><br>When people want to relax and they don't want to go to the movies. |

**Figure 3.5.** Fifth-grade students' responses to a Whyzit Cube game about novels.

## Topic: Baseball

| 1. What are the main purposes of the Whyzit? What are the most important things it is supposed to do or be used for? | 2. What is an unusual purpose of the Whyzit? How could the Whyzit be applied or used in an unusual way? |
|---|---|
| It's supposed to make you have team spirit, have fun, make friends, and get you some exercise, too. | It can teach cooperation. Maybe if two kids don't get along, you could make them play on the same team. |
| 3. When would it be wrong to use the Whyzit? When would it be misapplied or out of place? Explain.<br><br>In a museum or in a library. Too much noise, and stuff would get broken. | 4. All players: Brainstorm at least four ways to change the Whyzit to make it better, more interesting, or more effective. Be imaginative!<br><br>Have more positions, so more people could play.<br><br>Make wider bats, so more people could hit the ball.<br><br>Make the field bigger so there aren't so many home runs.<br><br>Make tickets cheaper, so more people could go watch pro games. |
| 5. How well does the Whyzit work? List two reasons why the Whyzit works well and two reasons why the Whyzit might need improvement. Ask the player on your left for help.<br><br>Works well: It can give people a nice career if they're good enough at it, and it does help you have fun and meet friends.<br><br>Needs improvement: Not many penalties for poor sportsmanship, and it's too slow sometimes. | 6. Identify two examples of the Whyzit in action. Think of situations, instances, or places where people use or apply the Whyzit.<br><br>People use Little League baseball to get their kids out doing something after school with other kids.<br><br>In softball, the rules are the same but you use a bigger ball. |

**Figure 3.6.** Fifth-grade students' responses to a Whyzit Cube game about baseball.

## Topic: Civilization

| | |
|---|---|
| **1. What are the main purposes of the Whyzit? What are the most important things it is supposed to do or be used for?**<br><br>It brings people together in communities.<br><br>Best way to have enough food and products for everyone.<br><br>Allows "special" jobs like lawyers, artists, and judges to come about. | **2. What is an unusual purpose of the Whyzit? How could the Whyzit be applied or used in an unusual way?**<br><br>It could be used to get everybody to contribute, not just a few people in the community.<br><br>It could be used with religion to help people get along and survive together. |
| **3. When would it be wrong to use the Whyzit? When would it be misapplied or out of place? Explain.**<br><br>We wouldn't need civilizations where resources are unlimited, or in places where not many people live and have to compete for resources. | **4. All players: Brainstorm at least four ways to change the Whyzit to make it better, more interesting, or more effective. Be imaginative!**<br><br>If schools taught more languages so we can communicate with more people.<br><br>If more people were better educated.<br><br>If we set up more community-based governments instead of one big one away from communities.<br><br>If it had more recreation to bring people together. |
| **5. How well does the Whyzit work? List two reasons why the Whyzit works well and two reasons why the Whyzit might need improvement. Ask the player on your left for help.**<br><br>Works well: Because there is less death and crime in civilizations.<br><br>Needs improvement: Because there is still unemployment problems and overpopulation in many civilizations. | **6. Identify two examples of the Whyzit in action. Think of situations, instances, or places where people use or apply the Whyzit.**<br><br>The United States. We have lots of resources and lots of people, so we need to be civilized about it.<br><br>Japan. They have a civilization that's different from ours, but it seems to work. |

**Figure 3.7.** Eighth-grade students' responses to a Whyzit Cube game about civilization.

## Topic: Computer animation

| 1. What are the main purposes of the Whyzit? What are the most important things it is supposed to do or be used for? | 2. What is an unusual purpose of the Whyzit? How could the Whyzit be applied or used in an unusual way? |
|---|---|
| Lets you use your imagination and express yourself and your ideas or a message in other ways than writing or speaking. | It might be used by Special Education teachers as a way to get kids to enjoy whatever subject they're studying. |
| It's another way to communicate with a broad range of audiences. | It could be used to provide learning opportunities for people who are visual learners. |
| **3. When would it be wrong to use the Whyzit? When would it be misapplied or out of place? Explain.** | **4. All players: Brainstorm at least four ways to change the Whyzit to make it better, more interesting, or more effective. Be imaginative!** |
| Sometimes animation can trivialize things and send the wrong message. So it might not be good to use it to talk about serious topics like drug use, maybe, or political ads for candidates. | Make it more realistic, the more realistic the better, without making it look artificial or computerized. |
| | It'd be better if we could add music to it. |
| | Some animation would be better if it used more text or subtitles. |
| | If it could be used more in the classroom to help teach students new topics. |
| **5. How well does the Whyzit work? List two reasons why the Whyzit works well and two reasons why the Whyzit might need improvement. Ask the player on your left for help.** | **6. Identify two examples of the Whyzit in action. Think of situations, instances, or places where people use or apply the Whyzit.** |
| Works well: It's entertaining and an attention grabber, and it makes an impression on an audience. | In a movie theater or TV studio. |
| | In an advertising company to make commercials. |
| Needs improvement: It doesn't give a perfect image; trivializes topics; adults usually aren't impressed by it. | In training videos for schools or in computer businesses that produce new software products and games. |

**Figure 3.8.** Twelfth-grade students' responses to a Whyzit Cube game about computer animation.

## *Where to Go from Here: Planning Future Lessons*

The Whyzit Cube addresses the questions What is it for? and How does it work? To design lessons that take students' thinking about these questions even further, ask yourself the following questions as you review students' responses:

- What kinds of key and unusual purposes did students identify? Are the purposes they listed relevant to the topic? What do the responses indicate about students' understanding of the topic?

- How well did students identify examples of the topic in action? How workable were the examples? Did they make sense? Were they creative or probing?

- What kinds of evaluations of the Whyzit did students make? Were their evaluations relevant? Balanced?

To help you think about possible future lessons, here are two stories that illustrate how you might conduct follow-up lessons to the Whyzit game.

### Explaining by Example and Application

Mr. Kersey had just started a unit on democracy with his sixth-grade class. He wanted his students to understand not only the key principles of democracy but also to identify examples of democracy in action. Even though he was just beginning the unit, Mr. Kersey knew that students already had a bit of prior knowledge about democracy, so he put students into small groups and had them play the Whyzit Cube game.

When students finished playing the game, Mr. Kersey collected the response sheets. Right away, he noticed that two of the groups had left challenge 6 blank. (Challenge 6 asks for examples of the Whyzit in action.) All of the other groups had answered the question with the same response: "The United States." Mr. Kersey asked the groups what had happened. "We couldn't think of any examples of democracy in action, except for our own government," students said.

Mr. Kersey decided to push students' thinking a little harder. He decided to put challenge 6 to the class as a whole. So he asked students again: "What are some examples of democracy in action?"

"Be creative," he urged. "Go beyond thinking about the United States. Think of other kinds of examples." He paused for a moment. "Not just countries," he added. "Think of your own daily lives. Remember, one of the principles of democracy is that it is *the people*—not just one class or one person or a special group—who make decisions about how things should be run. Another principle is government by elected representation. This means we the people elect representatives to take active part in the process of governance. And another principle is natural rights—the idea that there are certain inalienable rights that all people have and that government is required to respect." Mr. Kersey paused, and then went on. "Can any of you think of examples of any of these principles in your own lives?"

"Sometimes in school we vote," one student said. "Voting is a way of getting everyone's opinion, so I guess that's democracy."

"My father's on the School Committee," another student said. "And people had voted for him to be there. So I guess that's democracy, since, when it comes to education, the School Committee makes decisions for everyone in town."

Mr. Kersey wrote both responses on the blackboard. "Any other ideas?" he asked.

At least 10 seconds of silence passed, then a student said: "I don't know if this fits, but sometimes at dinner my younger sister tries to say something and my older sister interrupts her. Then my younger sister tells my older sister to be quiet, and that she has a right to her own opinion. Is that an example of natural rights?"

Mr. Kersey paused for a minute, then said: "Sounds like your younger sister thinks it's an example of the right to freedom of speech." And he wrote the idea on the board.

The brainstorm continued. Mr. Kersey continued to write down students' ideas and inwardly congratulated himself for pushing students to think more deeply about this question. Remembering the curriculum, he was quite pleased that the Bill of Rights was scheduled to be the topic for tomorrow's class.

## Seeking Key and Hidden Purposes

Ms. Abbott's fifth graders were learning how to do long division during math class when she got the idea to use the Whyzit Cube game. Although most of her students had little trouble following the mechanical steps of long division, Ms. Abbott sensed that students didn't really understand the purpose of division as a mathematical function.

As Ms. Abbott reviewed the Whyzit response sheets, she observed that an overwhelming number of students seemed to have only a fuzzy notion of the purpose of division. One student wrote that the purpose of division was "to double check if a multiplication problem is right, even if it has remainders." Another said the purpose of division was "to divide things into parts." A few students seemed to hit closer to the mark. For example, one student observed, "The purpose of division is to make a system for grouping numbers into parts." Not satisfied with her students' overall understanding of division, she decided to revise her math lesson for the next day.

Knowing that teaching another person is one of the best ways to get at the essence of a topic, Ms. Abbott wrote the problem $354 \div 16$ on the board. Then she asked students to write down on paper how they would teach a person who didn't know long division how to do the problem.

After students had been writing for about 10 minutes, Ms. Abbott stopped the class and asked students to read the explanation they had written to a partner. Then she asked them to turn back to their papers and answer the following questions: What seemed good about your explanation of division? What about division was difficult to explain? After students had written their answers, Ms. Abbott revisited challenge 1 from the day before. She said, "Take a moment to think again about challenge 1 from yesterday's game. What are the purposes of division? Write down any new ideas you have." Several students furrowed their brows, but, after a moment or two, all students were busily writing. Ms. Abbott leaned back in her chair, watched her students at work, and looked forward to reading their papers.

# Causal
# Tic-Tac-Toe

## How Causal Tic-Tac-Toe Cultivates
## Critical Thinking and Understanding

Understanding causality—the relationship between cause and effect—is fundamental to our understanding of the world. It comes as no surprise, then, that an understanding of causality is the focus of many topics in the curriculum. For example, we want students to be able to explain such things as what caused the actions of historical and literary figures; what causes natural phenomena, such as plant growth or wave action; what causes contemporary social problems; and so on. All of these situations have complex causes—causes that come from many sources and exert various kinds of influences. Yet people often go wrong when they think about causality because they construct overly simplistic causal explanations—explanations that identify only one or two causes or that regard causality as a step-by-step, linear process rather than as a dynamic and interacting process.

Constructing accurate, complex causal explanations requires good critical thinking. This is because understanding causality involves such skills as evaluating the relative importance of contributing causes, understanding the various relationships among causes, and looking broadly for different types of causes. The game of Causal Tic-Tac-Toe is designed to help students think critically in these ways. Specifically, it helps to deepen students' understanding of causality by challenging them to

- **Identify multiple causes.** Causal Tic-Tac-Toe challenges students to go beyond simplistic explanations to seek several causes for an occurrence, including causes that come from various sources.

- **Distinguish between a cause and a noncausal correlation.** Often, people go wrong thinking about causality because they mistake events that happen to occur sequentially or simultaneously as having a causal relationship. Causal Tic-Tac-Toe helps students identify the difference between a cause and an unrelated correlation.

- **Distinguish between simultaneous and sequential causes.** Some causes are part of a chain of events; other causes occur simultaneously with one another. Causal Tic-Tac-Toe helps students to make this distinction.

- **Explore the difference between sufficient and possible causes.** Some causes exert enough influence to guarantee a certain effect. Other causes may possibly produce certain effects, but are not sufficient to guarantee them. Causal Tic-Tac-Toe helps students explore the difference between sufficient and possible causes.

These four skills require students to understand some important technical concepts involved in causal reasoning, concepts like *correlation* and *sufficient cause*. Figure 4.1 explains the technical terminology and gives examples of causal reasoning. If you wonder whether these terms and concepts are too difficult for students to understand, refer to the sample student responses in figures 4.5–4.8 (pages 78–81). We have found that, with occasional guidance from the teacher, students catch on quickly.

## What Is a Cause?

A cause is something that produces an effect. It is an occurrence that precedes and helps to bring about another action or event. We use the word *cause* all the time. Here are some examples:

- Water causes plants to grow.

- The full moon causes high tides.

- Pop quizzes often cause stress!

- Earthworms cause the soil to be aerated.

- Kids with in-line skates sometimes cause pedestrians to be alarmed.

- An abundance of natural resources often causes nations to prosper.

- Smoking causes cancer.

## What Is an Effect?

An effect is an occurrence that is the result of one or several causes. For example, if smoking causes cancer, then cancer is an *effect* of smoking. If the full moon causes especially high tides, then especially high tides are an *effect* of the full moon.

Just to make things confusing, it is important to recognize that an occurrence can be an effect of one thing and a cause of something else at the same time. Take smoking. Cancer is an *effect* of smoking. And cancer is (sometimes) a *cause* of death. So, cancer is both an effect (of smoking) and a cause (of death). Or, take tides and the moon. Especially high tides are an *effect* of the full moon. Especially high tides can also be a *cause* of flooding.

**Figure 4.1.** Definitions for Causal Tic-Tac-Toe.

## *Many Things Have Several Causes*

Lots of things have more than one cause. For example, consider pollution. Many things can contribute to causing pollution, such as the burning of fossil fuel, improper waste disposal, governmental policies, people's attitudes, and even natural occurrences like earthquakes and floods.

## *Sequential Causes*

Sometimes, when something has several causes, the causes are sequential, that is, they follow each other one by one in sequence. For example, suppose you woke up one morning and discovered that the road outside your home was flooded. What caused it to be flooded? Well, it rained a lot last night, and the rain caused the river to rise. Eventually, the river overflowed its banks and flooded the road. The causes of the flooded road followed each other one by one: First it rained; then the banks of the river overflowed onto the road. These are *sequential causes.*

## *Simultaneous Causes*

Sometimes when something has several causes, two or more causes occur at the same time. In the previous example, suppose the river that overflowed happened to be near an ocean and was, therefore, affected by the ocean tides. (Ocean tides "back up" a certain distance into rivers that empty into the ocean.) Now suppose that, on the night of the rainstorm the moon was full. Tides are always especially high during a full moon. Suppose that the rain wasn't quite enough to make the river overflow its banks, and neither was the high tide. Neither cause, by itself, was enough to cause the flood. But together, the especially high tide and the rain were enough to make the river overflow. Both the rainstorm *and* the high tide had to happen at the same time to cause the flood. So, the especially high tide and the rain are *simultaneous causes* of the flood.

**Figure 4.1.** Definitions for Causal Tic-Tac-Toe (continued).

## Sufficient Causes

A sufficient cause guarantees that an effect will occur. For example, plants need water to live. If you don't water a houseplant, it will die. Not watering the plant is *sufficient cause* for the plant to die.

Sometimes, an event can have more than one sufficient cause. Think about this:

At the very least, plants need both light and water. Take away either one, and the plant dies. If you don't water a plant, it will die. But that's not the only way to kill a plant. Another way is to put the plant in a closet where it doesn't get any light. Even if you water it, the plant in the closet will die. Either cause—no light *or* no water—by itself, guarantees the plant will die. Thus, not watering a plant is one *sufficient cause* for the plant's death, and putting the plant in a closet is another, separate *sufficient cause* for the plant's death.

When are causes not sufficient? Take the example of the flooded road. Neither the rainstorm nor the high tides were, in themselves enough to cause the flood. Both had to happen at the same time (simultaneously) to cause the flood. Neither the rain nor the high tide, taken alone, were *sufficient causes* of the flood.

## Possible Causes

A possible cause is something that may—but doesn't always—produce a certain effect. Take smoking, for example. Many smokers suffer from cancer or heart disease. But not *all* smokers suffer from these diseases. On the other hand, some people who have never smoked come down with cancer or heart disease. So, smoking is a *possible* cause of smoking and heart disease.

**Figure 4.1.** Definitions for Causal Tic-Tac-Toe (continued).

## *Correlations Are Not Causes*

Sometimes two or more events accompany one another but don't cause each other. These are *correlations*. Here are two examples:

Presidents of countries tend to be tall. But being tall doesn't cause you to be president. Nor does being president cause you to be tall. Height and presidency are correlated.

People who smoke cigarettes also tend to bite their fingernails. But smoking doesn't cause you to bite your nails, nor does biting your nails cause you to smoke. Smoking and nail biting are correlated.

Sometimes, two things that are correlated may be caused by the same thing. For example, being under a lot of stress might cause you to smoke and to bite your nails. But smoking and nail biting don't cause each other.

**Figure 4.1.** Definitions for Causal Tic-Tac-Toe (continued).

## When to Use Causal Tic-Tac-Toe

**Use Causal Tic-Tac-Toe in the middle or toward the end of a unit to help students understand a key historical, literary, or contemporary event.**

Many topics in the curriculum are centered around an important event. For example, it might be a key historical moment, such as the signing of the Declaration of Independence or the 1964 March on Washington. It might be a contemporary event, such as a rise in gang violence or a decision to build a new community center. Or, it might be the development of a literary style or genre, such as the detective novel. Events that are central to the curriculum typically have several contributing causes, and exploring their causal structure helps students understand the event and its significance more deeply.

**Use Causal Tic-Tac-Toe to explore causal situations that have several contributing causes.**

Keep in mind that Causal Tic-Tac-Toe helps students explore and understand complex causal situations. So try to choose a situation that has several contributing causes, that is, causes that come from several different sources and that exert various kinds of causal influences. An easy way to tell whether a causal situation is a good candidate for Causal Tic-Tac-Toe is to try it out yourself, first. Imagine how the questions in the game apply to a causal scenario you are considering, and see how interesting the answers seem to be.

## Getting Started

1. Choose a causal question or scenario. Following are some examples of causal questions:

   - What geographic conditions cause a volcano?

   - What human–environment interactions cause pollution?

   - What political and social events caused the Magna Carta (or Declaration of Independence or Bill of Rights) to be written?

   - What caused the French Revolution?

   - What causes competitiveness?

   - What causes ocean waves?

   - What caused the Civil War?

   - What causes social intolerance?

   - What causes people to change their moods?

   - What causes people to be explorers?

   - What caused the great tide of immigration into the United States in the early 1900s?

   - What caused Huck Finn to run away from home?

   - What causes students to drop out of school?

- What causes people to speak in various dialects?

- What causes kids to join gangs?

- What causes people to start smoking?

- What causes people to form communities?

- What causes racism?

- What causes plant growth?

2. Schedule a time for students to play Causal Tic-Tac-Toe. (See the When to Use Causal Tic-Tac-Toe section of this chapter for more suggestions about when to use the game.) Typically, a game takes about 15–25 minutes to play. Most teachers introduce the game at the middle or toward the end of a unit of study.

3. Group students into pairs or groups of four. If students are in groups of four, have them play in teams of two against two. Give each group

   - a copy of the definitions handout (figure 4.1)

   - a Causal Tic-Tac-Toe master game piece (figure 4.2)

   - a Response Sheet (figure 4.3)

4. Explain the rules aloud. Either post the rules where students can easily refer to them, or give each group a copy. (See figure 4.4 for rules.)

5. Review the definitions aloud and model how they are used when playing the game. Do this by choosing a causal situation that students are familiar with, then asking and answering aloud the Tic-Tac-Toe questions, referring to the definitions handout when appropriate.

6. Remind groups to record their responses on the Response Sheet. Collect the sheets when students are done. If you wish, provide written or verbal feedback using the Guidelines for Feedback in this chapter.

7. See the Where to Go from Here section of this chapter for suggestions about how to follow up Causal Tic-Tac-Toe in planning future lessons.

All players: Describe the effect, that is, the situation or event for which you are seeking causes.

| | | |
|---|---|---|
| Identify two causes that influence each other. | Can you think of two different *kinds* of causes—ones that come from very different sources? | All players: Brainstorm all of the possible causes. Time limit: 1 minute. |
| Identify two causes that could occur *sequentially.* (Causes that occur one after the other.) | Identify two causes that could occur *simultaneously.* (Causes that occur at the same time.) | List one thing that might look like a cause, but might really be a *correlation.* (Something that occurs at the same time but isn't a cause.) |
| Can you think of a possible hidden cause—a cause that might exist but that we don't see right now? | Which causes, if any, are *sufficient* causes? (Causes that guarantee the effect will occur.) | Which causes are *possible* causes? (Things that *might* cause the effect to occur but don't guarantee that it will.) |

**Figure 4.2.** Causal Tic-Tac-Toe master game sheet.

# Causal Tic-Tac-Toe Response Sheet

All players: Describe the effect, that is, the situation or event for which you are seeking causes.

_____

Names: _____

_____

**Challenge 1**
Identify two causes that influence each other.

**Challenge 2**
Can you think of two different _kinds_ of causes—ones that come from very different sources?

**Figure 4.3.** Causal Tic-Tac-Toe Response Sheet.

From _Critical Squares: Games of Critical Thinking and Understanding._ © 1997.
Teacher Ideas Press 1-800-237-6124.

## Causal Tic-Tac-Toe Response Sheet (continued)

**Challenge 3**

All players: Brainstorm all of the possible causes. Time limit: 1 minute.

**Figure 4.3.** Causal Tic-Tac-Toe Response Sheet (continued).

## Causal Tic-Tac-Toe Response Sheet (continued)

**Challenge 4**
Identify two causes that could occur *sequentially.* (Causes that occur one after the other.)

**Challenge 5**
Identify two causes that could occur *simultaneously.* (Causes that occur at the same time.)

**Figure 4.3.** Causal Tic-Tac-Toe Response Sheet (continued).

## Causal Tic-Tac-Toe Response Sheet (continued)

**Challenge 6**

List one thing that might look like a cause, but might really be a *correlation*. (Something that occurs at the same time but isn't a cause.)

**Challenge 7**

Can you think of a possible hidden cause—a cause that might exist but that we don't see right now?

**Figure 4.3.** Causal Tic-Tac-Toe Response Sheet (continued).

## Causal Tic-Tac-Toe Response Sheet (continued)

**Challenge 8**
Which causes, if any, are *sufficient* causes? (Causes that guarantee the effect will occur.)

**Challenge 9**
Which causes are *possible* causes? (Things that *might* cause the effect to occur but don't guarantee that it will.)

**Figure 4.3.** Causal Tic-Tac-Toe Response Sheet (continued).

# Rules of Causal Tic-Tac-Toe

*For two players or two teams of players.*

1. Each player or team tries to fill three squares in a row (horizontal, vertical, or diagonal). The first team or player to do so wins the game.

2. To fill a square, the player or team must fully answer the question in the corresponding square on the master game sheet.

3. All answers must be written on the Response Sheet.

4. Before writing an answer on the Response Sheet, all players on both teams must agree that the answer is acceptable. If full agreement can't be reached, all players must vote. If there are only two players, and they disagree about the acceptability of an answer, or if the vote among the teams is a tie, an outside person must be asked to decide. If an answer is judged to be unacceptable, the team or player may try to answer the question one more time.

   If the second response a team makes is also judged unacceptable, the team loses its turn and the square remains blank.

**Figure 4.4.** Rules of Causal Tic-Tac-Toe.

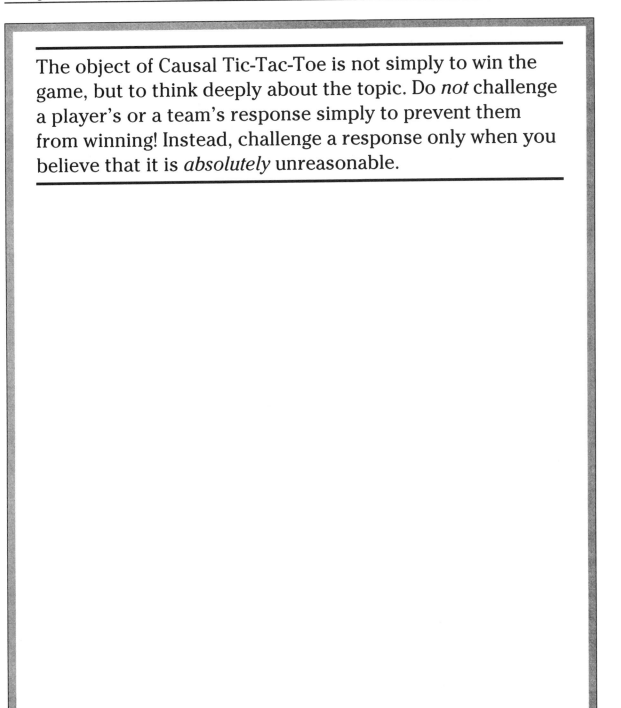

The object of Causal Tic-Tac-Toe is not simply to win the game, but to think deeply about the topic. Do *not* challenge a player's or a team's response simply to prevent them from winning! Instead, challenge a response only when you believe that it is *absolutely* unreasonable.

**Figure 4.4.** Rules of Causal Tic-Tac-Toe (continued).

## Sample Student Responses

Thinking about causality is challenging, but it comes naturally to most students. This is because most students are naturally curious about where things come from and what causes things to be the way they are.

Figures 4.5–4.8 give examples of responses students produced while playing Causal Tic-Tac-Toe. As you read through the examples, keep in mind that they were collected from students who were playing the game for the first time. The students were not coached by us or their teachers, but they show a remarkable ability to reason about complex causal situations.

## Guidelines for Feedback: Responding to Students' Thinking

It is challenging to think broadly about the variety of causal influences on an event, and it is challenging to understand the complex interactions of causes. However, understanding complex cause-and-effect situations is a key dimension of understand subject matter, and the ability to engage in causal reasoning is a key critical thinking ability. So causal reasoning is especially worth teaching, and it is especially important to support students' learning by providing them with frequent and informative feedback about their work.

Many students' answers to the questions in Causal Tic-Tac-Toe will fall into the following four categories:

- Identifying several causes of an event or situation, including different kinds of causes

- Exploring the difference between a cause and a correlation

- Identifying relationships among causes (i.e., sequential, simultaneous, interacting)

- Exploring the difference between sufficient causes and possible causes

Following are things to look for and respond to in each category, along with examples drawn from actual student responses.

### Identifying Causes and Kinds of Causes

Identify and commend responses that...

indicate opposing or contrasting perspectives, recognize alternative explanations, classify causes by type or kind, look beyond the obvious cause or explanation.

**Examples**

*One kind of cause comes from inside the person, another kind of cause comes from the outside world (environment, surroundings, etc.).*

*Competition in students is caused by parents, peer pressure, a desire to win, wanting to feel good about yourself.*

*Pollution is caused by things left over from years ago and also by things happening right now.*

## Differentiating Cause and Correlation

Identify and commend responses that...

show understanding of the relative contribution of factors and influences; distinguish between connected and unconnected factors.

**Examples**

*It's a sunny day and you get an A on your paper. I'd be in a good mood because of the A, no matter what the weather was.*

*A river might be polluted, and there might be a new housing development on it. But that doesn't mean building the houses caused the pollution.*

## Identifying Relationships Among Causes

Identify and commend responses that...

link factors or causes, recognize the influences of causes on one another, organize causes logically, consider time and placement of causes in relation to an event, make connections between seemingly disparate causes.

**Examples**

*Explorers explore because they might want to be rich and they want to discover new things.*

*Rivers get polluted because people bury toxic waste, then the soil runs into the river and pollutes the river.*

*People's surroundings and how much time they spend in those surroundings can cause changes in their moods.*

## Differentiating Sufficient and Possible Causes

Identify and commend responses that...

distinguish causes that guarantee certain outcomes from those that don't; recognize absolute connections between a cause and an event.

**Examples**

*A possible cause for wanting to explore is if somebody wanted to get famous or rich.*

*Burning fossil fuels in cars and trucks guarantees more air pollution.*

*A possible cause for changing moods is if you flunk a test or someone gives you a hug.*

# What causes people to be explorers?

| | | |
|---|---|---|
| **Identify two causes that influence each other.**<br><br>The explorers might want to get rich.<br><br>They might want to discover new things. | **Can you think of two different _kinds_ of causes—ones that come from very different sources?**<br><br>One kind is from what they feel like doing, and another is from what other people tell them to do. | **All players: Brainstorm all of the possible causes. Time limit: 1 minute.**<br><br>Greed<br>Fame<br>New foods and spices<br>Bored at home<br>Religion<br>Forced into it<br>New weapons |
| **Identify two causes that could occur _sequentially._ (Causes that occur one after the other.)**<br><br>People lose their jobs and then they realize that they need to go out there and make more money. | **Identify two causes that could occur _simultaneously._ (Causes that occur at the same time.)**<br><br>Someone could be thinking about going exploring, when a friend calls him and asks him to go exploring. | **List one thing that might look like a cause, but might really be a _correlation._ (Something that occurs at the same time but isn't a cause.)**<br><br>Explorers like new things and excitement. |
| **Can you think of a possible hidden cause—a cause that might exist but that we don't see right now?**<br><br>Explorers like to be first at finding new things out. | **Which causes, if any, are _sufficient_ causes? (Causes that guarantee the effect will occur.)**<br><br>A sufficient cause is that they had to be thinking about exploring in the first place. | **Which causes are _possible_ causes? (Things that _might_ cause the effect to occur but don't guarantee that it will.)**<br><br>If somebody wanted to get famous or rich. |

**Figure 4.5.** Fifth-grade students' responses to a Causal Tic-Tac-Toe game about "What causes people to be explorers?"

# What causes competitiveness?

| Identify two causes that influence each other. | Can you think of two different *kinds* of causes—ones that come from very different sources? | All players: Brainstorm all of the possible causes. Time limit: 1 minute. |
|---|---|---|
| Past experience and how hard you try. Whatever happened in the past can influence how competitive you are. | Causes from outside, like peer pressure, and causes from inside, like how much self-esteem you have. | Parents<br>What you're good at<br>Desire to win<br>Feel good about yourself<br>To show off<br>Pressure from friends<br>Not let people or team down |
| **Identify two causes that could occur *sequentially*. (Causes that occur one after the other.)** | **Identify two causes that could occur *simultaneously*. (Causes that occur at the same time.)** | **List one thing that might look like a cause, but might really be a *correlation*. (Something that occurs at the same time but isn't a cause.)** |
| First, you could fail at something, and then all of a sudden there's lots of pressure to do well at it next time, like a test, so you try twice as hard to do well. | You could be working for a common goal with your team, like winning a game. And you can hear the crowd cheering at the same time. | It might seem like kids are competitive when their parents get all psyched up, but maybe kids just want to win on their own. |
| **Can you think of a possible hidden cause—a cause that might exist but that we don't see right now?** | **Which causes, if any, are *sufficient* causes? (Causes that guarantee the effect will occur.)** | **Which causes are *possible* causes? (Things that *might* cause the effect to occur but don't guarantee that it will.)** |
| A hidden cause might be that we are taught to be competitive now, so we can compete later in life, on jobs or whatever. | Winning. If it's the most important thing, then you'll be competitive. | If you want to succeed at something. You may want it, like good grades, but not really try for it. |

**Figure 4.6.** Eighth-grade students' responses to a Causal Tic-Tac-Toe game about "What causes competitiveness?"

# What causes pollution?

| **Identify two causes that influence each other.**<br><br>Water supplies get polluted because contaminated soil runs into the rivers, but farmers need to use chemicals and fertilizer on the land. | **Can you think of two different *kinds* of causes—ones that come from very different sources?**<br><br>Causes that are left over from years ago, and causes that are happening right now. | **All players: Brainstorm all of the possible causes. Time limit: 1 minute.**<br><br>Improper storage of materials<br>Burning fossil fuels<br>Illegal dumping<br>Laziness<br>Farming near delicate resources<br>Cutting down forests<br>Travel |
|---|---|---|
| **Identify two causes that could occur *sequentially.* (Causes that occur one after the other.)**<br><br>Burying toxic waste pollutes the soil, and then the toxic soil pollutes rivers and drinking water. | **Identify two causes that could occur *simultaneously.* (Causes that occur at the same time.)**<br><br>Somebody could be dumping illegally, while other people are littering on the other side of town. | **List one thing that might look like a cause, but might really be a *correlation.* (Something that occurs at the same time but isn't a cause.)**<br><br>A river might be polluted, and there might be a new housing development on it. But that doesn't mean building the houses caused the pollution. |
| **Can you think of a possible hidden cause—a cause that might exist but that we don't see right now?**<br><br>There could be chemical reactions in the atmosphere we haven't noticed yet. | **Which causes, if any, are *sufficient* causes? (Causes that guarantee the effect will occur.)**<br><br>Burning fossil fuels in cars and trucks guarantees more air pollution. | **Which causes are *possible* causes? (Things that *might* cause the effect to occur but don't guarantee that it will.)**<br><br>Farming doesn't guarantee pollution of the water supplies, but it can. |

**Figure 4.7.** Eighth-grade students' responses to a Causal Tic-Tac-Toe game about "What causes pollution?"

# What causes people to change their moods?

| | | |
|---|---|---|
| **Identify two causes that influence each other.**<br><br>People's surroundings can be one cause, and how much time they spend in those surroundings can influence their moods. | **Can you think of two different *kinds* of causes—ones that come from very different sources?**<br><br>One kind of cause comes from inside the person, and another kind of cause comes from the outside world. | **All players: Brainstorm all of the possible causes. Time limit: 1 minute.**<br><br>Other people's moods<br>Lack of sleep<br>Bad diet<br>The weather<br>The time of day<br>Amount of pressure that day (e.g., test)<br>How well I'm doing at school or work |
| **Identify two causes that could occur *sequentially*. (Causes that occur one after the other.)**<br><br>What I'm thinking about puts me in one mood already, and then someone says something and I react to it. | **Identify two causes that could occur *simultaneously*. (Causes that occur at the same time.)**<br><br>Two people can be arguing with you at the same time, and they both make you angry. | **List one thing that might look like a cause, but might really be a *correlation*. (Something that occurs at the same time but isn't a cause.)**<br><br>It's a sunny day and you get an A on your paper. I'd be in a good mood because of the A no matter what the weather was. |
| **Can you think of a possible hidden cause—a cause that might exist but that we don't see right now?**<br><br>The environment could be a hidden cause. Maybe there's something in the air or in the water that makes people feel sick or whatever and it changes their mood. | **Which causes, if any, are *sufficient* causes? (Causes that guarantee the effect will occur.)**<br><br>I don't know if there are any. Everybody reacts differently to things. You can't predict how someone's mood is going to change, because there is always an exception. | **Which causes are *possible* causes? (Things that *might* cause the effect to occur but don't guarantee that it will.)**<br><br>If you flunk a test or if someone gives you a hug might be things that could change your mood, but they might not. |

**Figure 4.8.** Twelfth-grade students' responses to a Causal Tic-Tac-Toe game about "What causes people to change their moods?"

## *Where to Go from Here: Planning Future Lessons*

You can help students learn to more effectively reason about causes by asking yourself the following questions:

- Which aspects of Causal Tic-Tac-Toe did your students easily understand? What does this tell you about their reasoning ability? What does it tell you about their understanding of the topic?

- Which aspects of Causal Tic-Tac-Toe were difficult or confusing for students? Why?

- What sorts of trends did you notice in students' thinking? How can you build on or remediate these trends in future lessons?

The following sample scenarios illustrate how a teacher could follow up on Causal Tic-Tac-Toe. Though the scenarios don't offer step-by-step instruction, they may give you a sense of the kind of follow-up lessons that are appropriate for your students.

### Creating Visual Aids to Understanding

Mr. Stephano's ninth-grade Western Civilization class played Causal Tic-Tac-Toe toward the end of a unit on the Roman Empire. Mr. Stephano knew that the so-called Fall of the Roman Empire was not a singular event, but rather a complex web of events and decisions. An objective for Mr. Stephano was to challenge his students to identify and analyze the many political and economic causes behind the fall of the empire and explore the relationships among those causes.

Later, Mr. Stephano reviewed his students' responses. Generally, he liked what he read. But he remained unsure of whether students actually had a clear picture of how the events and circumstances influenced and related to each other. So, being a visual learner himself, he designed a follow-up lesson in which students would construct a causal web, a giant graphic organizer that could be used to structure the causal connections and relationships into a visible reference.

The next day, small groups of students used their responses from Causal Tic-Tac-Toe to begin sketching rough drafts of time lines, flowcharts, and webs. As students sketched, Mr. Stephano realized that the feedback guidelines for Causal Tic-Tac-Toe were also appropriate in this lesson. So as he circulated the classroom reviewing students' work, he urged students to look for a variety of causes, to distinguish between causes and correlations, to think about sufficient and possible causes, and so on.

As it happened, students began to think so deeply about the causal relationship involved in the fall of the Roman Empire that the follow-up lesson extended into the next period. But Mr. Stephano was glad to let it happen, because he knew his students were gaining a deeper understanding not only of historical events but also about the complex nature of causality.

## What Ms. Burke Did

Ms. Burke, a junior high school health teacher, was in the middle of teaching a unit on the immune system. She and her seventh graders were learning about B-cells, T-cells, bacteria, viruses, antibodies, and other topics related to the immune system, when one of her students asked, "What causes us to get sick?" Other students expressed an interest in the question as well. Seizing the opportunity to encourage students to think critically about causal relationships, she arranged her students into small groups and distributed the Causal Tic-Tac-Toe game.

As students played the game, Ms. Burke assisted individual groups as necessary. While circulating from group to group, she noticed some confusion among students about the difference between cause and correlation. Ms. Burke described some of the distinctions between cause and correlation to the class, but she sensed her students still were not clear about the two concepts. For example, one group had listed "chicken soup" as a possible cause, reasoning that because people often eat chicken soup when they have a cold, it might be part of the cause. While developing lesson plans for the next day, Ms. Burke decided she needed to address the issue with a follow-up lesson.

When students entered her class the following day, they discovered that Ms. Burke had listed on the board all the causes they had brainstormed while playing Causal Tic-Tac-Toe. She asked students to review the list and create a "causes and correlations" chart for the common cold. She asked, "Which of the ideas listed might contribute to *causing* a cold? Which of the ideas on the board might be *associated* with catching a cold, but not necessarily be part of its cause?" Ms. Burke placed a transparency she had created from the Definitions Page of the Causal Tic-Tac-Toe chapter on the overhead projector, and reviewed the definitions of cause and correlation with the class. She used the chicken soup example to illustrate the difference between the concepts of cause and correlation.

Naturally, students suggested several ideas that were hard to classify, such as "not wearing a hat." Some students argued that not wearing a hat in chilly weather was something that causes people to catch colds. Others countered that not wearing a hat was more of a myth than a cause. Ms. Burke added a column to the chart and labeled it "Unsure," then wrote "not wearing a hat" under it. She wanted to show her students that sometimes, distinguishing between causes and correlations can be tricky.

# 5

# The Connection Cube Game

# How the Connection Cube Cultivates
## Critical Thinking and Understanding

Arguably, the most important job of education is to provide students with knowledge that they can transfer in meaningful ways to other aspects of their present or future lives. For example, we do not teach history simply so students can pass a quiz, but so that they can reason better about the world around them. We do not teach mathematics so that students can continue to do math exercises, but so that they can use mathematics in their personal and professional lives.

Yet research has shown that the transfer of knowledge does not happen nearly as much as we would like. Too often, students do not make the connections they should between new knowledge and prior knowledge, between one school subject and another, between school learning and everyday life.

Transfer, or making connections, is an important part of critical thinking and understanding because it involves actively constructing new knowledge out of old. That is, it involves inventing, adapting, and critiquing the application of prior knowledge to new contexts. Making connections can be quite creative, drawing on analogies and leaps of imagination, such as when a poet makes a connection between a smile and a summer moon. And it can be critical and evaluative, such as when we explore the connection between rules of chess and the rules of war or between the circulatory system of the body and the circulation of information in society.

Teachers who have used the Starting Block will notice some similarities between what the Starting Block and the Connection Cube do. This is because the Starting Block, too, is about making connections, but, because the Starting Block is used before students have plunged deeply into a topic, it emphasizes making connections to prior knowledge. The Connection Cube, on the other hand, helps students to make connections to new knowledge or seemingly unrelated areas of knowledge.

The Connection Cube encourages critical thinking and understanding in the following ways:

- **Identifying relevance.** By inviting students to make connections between the topic they are studying and other activities or areas of knowledge, the Connection Cube challenges students to identify the relevancy of what they are learning to the world at large.

- **Connecting to prior knowledge.** The Connection Cube challenges students to connect the content of what they are learning to prior knowledge they have about the world.

- **Transferring learning skills.** The Connection Cube challenges students to reflect on their learning process and to make connections between the learning they are now doing and past learning experiences.

- **Understanding the shape of the topic.** By asking students to identify what new ideas they have about the topic and what they could do to learn more about it, the Connection Cube helps students better understand the shape of the topic and how it fits into their larger web of knowledge.

## *When to Use the Connection Cube*

**Use the Connection Cube as a concluding lesson in a topic or unit.**

Use the Connection Cube as you near the end of a topic or unit. Whatever the subject matter—astronomy, the Supreme Court, simple machines, the Great Depression, Mayan civilization, Beethoven, the Middle Ages, inventors, nuclear energy, fractions, the brain, the U.S. Constitution—the Connection Cube encourages students to transfer knowledge and think more deeply about the topics they are studying.

**Use the Connection Cube in the middle of a unit to help students see the relevance of a topic or concept.**

Learning is especially meaningful when the connections between the topic being studied and other aspects of the learner's life are clear and explicit. The Connection Cube encourages students to think broadly about the relevancy of the topic they are studying, pushing them to identify relevant connections to the world at large and to their own lives.

For example, suppose you are in the middle of a unit on the French Revolution. Your lessons are moving along, but you sense the material is too far removed from the lives of your students. Use the Connection Cube to establish links between the material and your students' lives and to renew students' curiosity about the topic.

## *Getting Started*

1. Choose a topic or concept you want students to connect to other areas of their lives, inside or outside of school.

2. Schedule a time for students to play the Connection Cube game. The game may be played at the middle or end of a unit or any time an important topic or concept warrants further investigation. Typically, a game takes about 15 minutes to play. (See the When to Use the Connection Cube section of this chapter for more suggestions about when to use the Connection Cube.)

3. Have students work in small groups, with 3–5 students in each group. Give each group

    ■ a Connection Cube master game piece, pre-assembled or to assemble themselves (pattern appears in figure 5.1)

    ■ a Response Sheet (figure 5.2)

4. Explain the rules aloud, and either post the rules somewhere where students can easily refer to them, or give each group a copy of the rules. (See figure 5.3 for rules.)

5. Remind group to record their responses on the Response Sheet as they play the game. Collect the sheets when the groups are done. If you wish, provide written or verbal feedback using the Guidelines for Feedback section of this chapter.

6. See the Where to Go from Here section of this chapter for suggestions about how to build on the Connection Cube in planning future lessons.

**1.**

List two new ideas you have about this topic that you didn't have before studying it.

**2.**

Ask each player in the group to name one activity or job in which knowing about this topic could be important.

**3.**

Make a connection between this topic and something else you know.

**4.**

As a group, list four things you could do to learn more about this topic.

**5.**

Imagine that this topic doesn't exist or never existed. Describe two ways that the world might be different. Ask the group for help.

**6.**

Compare learning about this topic to learning about something else, in or out of school. Ask any player for help.

*To assemble: Cut along the solid lines, fold on the dotted lines, and tape together to form a cube.*

**Figure 5.1.** The Connection Cube game piece.

From *Critical Squares: Games of Critical Thinking and Understanding.* © 1997.
Teacher Ideas Press 1-800-237-6124.

# Connection Cube Response Sheet

Topic: _____

Names: _____

_____

Record your responses for each roll of the Connection Cube. If the same challenge is rolled twice, just add the responses to the correct column.

**Challenge 1**

List two new ideas you have about this topic that you didn't have before studying it.

**Challenge 2**

Ask each player in the group to name one activity or job in which knowing about this topic could be important.

**Figure 5.2.** Connection Cube Response Sheet.

From *Critical Squares: Games of Critical Thinking and Understanding.* © 1997.
Teacher Ideas Press 1-800-237-6124.

## Connection Cube Response Sheet (continued)

**Challenge 3**

Make a connection between this topic and something else you know.

**Challenge 4**

As a group, list four things you could do to learn more about this topic.

**Figure 5.2.** Connection Cube Response Sheet (continued).

## Connection Cube Response Sheet (continued)

### Challenge 5

Imagine that this topic doesn't exist or never existed. Describe two ways that the world might be different. Ask the group for help.

### Challenge 6

Compare learning about this topic to learning about something else, in or out of school. Ask any player for help.

**Figure 5.2.** Connection Cube Response Sheet (continued).

# Rules of the Connection Cube Game

*For groups of 3–5 players.*

1. Players take turns rolling the die. Each player has one roll per turn. The player with the last birthday in the calendar year rolls first.

2. Roll the die and answer the thinking challenge that faces up. The player who rolls the die records his or her responses on the Connection Cube Response Sheet.

3. Go around the circle twice, so each player has two turns.

4. Some questions ask the whole group to respond. For group challenges, the player who rolls the die records the group's responses on the Response Sheet.

5. Sometimes, the same thinking challenge comes up two times in a row. If this happens, the player or group must respond to the challenge again. If the challenge comes up more than two times in a row, roll the die again for a new thinking challenge.

**Figure 5.3.** Rules of the Connection Cube game.

## Sample Student Responses

Like an unanchored ship, new knowledge is in danger of drifting away unless it is connected to something solid. Students understand things more deeply and retain them longer when they connect new ideas and concepts to things they already know. The Connection Cube encourages students to connect the new knowledge learned in class to other areas of knowledge, both inside and outside of school.

Figures 5.4–5.7 provide some responses students gave to the thinking challenges in the Connection Cube. The samples are drawn from real students in real classrooms. They cover four topic areas at four grade levels. To get an idea of the responses your students will give when they play the Connection Cube, take a look at how other students have responded to the game. Chances are, the responses generated by your students will be as varied and as rich as the responses provided in the examples.

## Guidelines for Feedback: Responding to Students' Thinking

It is important to provide students with supportive, informative feedback. As with the other *Critical Squares* games, we suggest you offer feedback that commends good ideas and at the same time explains the strengths and weaknesses of students' thinking.

The critical thinking that students do while playing the Connection Cube typically falls into the following three categories:

- Transferring or making connections

- Reflecting on the learning process

- Identifying relevance

As you provide feedback, identify and commend instances of good thinking in each of these areas. Following are some aspects of critical thinking to look for in each category, along with examples of actual student responses.

### Transferring or Making Connections

Identify and commend responses that...

> relate new concepts to something students already know about, address an issue from a new or unusual perspective, make analogies, compare and contrast, or raise issues or concerns to unrelated areas of interest or study.

**Examples**

*The pioneers along the Oregon Trail and people on the* Mayflower *were similar because both groups explored new territory.*

*The Westward Movement was like the Civil War in that lots of families were split up during both events.*

*If the pioneers on the Oregon trail were alive today, they'd probably be astronauts.*

## Reflecting on the Learning Process

Identify and commend responses that...

compare learning strategies applied to various topics or subjects, identify strengths or weaknesses in one's learning, apply a plan for improved learning to other areas, demonstrate honest self-assessment.

### Examples

*We used cooperative groups to learn about things in school the same way the colonists learned from the Indians.*

*It's kind of like reading Faulkner to learn about life down South. It's fiction, but you learn a lot about southern life.*

*People tend to identify with groups. Even in the worst conditions, people want to belong to something.*

## Identifying Relevance

Identify and commend responses that...

make connections across subject matters, show empathy for and understanding of other viewpoints, make connections to areas outside of school, seek links between a subject and one's prior knowledge.

### Examples

*Lots of families got split up during the Westward Movement, just like they did during the Civil War.*

*The colonists were a lot like us because they understood that they needed laws to maintain society.*

*The struggle the prisoners faced in the story are in many ways the same struggles people face every day at work or in school.*

## Topic: The Holocaust

| | |
|---|---|
| **1. List two new ideas you have about this topic that you didn't have before studying it.**<br><br>I didn't know the Nazis killed other people besides the Jewish people.<br><br>I didn't know some middle-aged people were saved from being killed so they could work in Nazi labor camps instead. | **2. Ask each player in the group to name one activity or job in which knowing about this topic could be important.**<br><br>Author<br>Teacher<br>Rabbi<br>Painter<br>Video and movie producers<br>All American citizens |
| **3. Make a connection between this topic and something else you know.**<br><br>This is like endangered animals that people round up and kill for no reason.<br><br>It reminded me of what extinction meant and why people want to make any species extinct. | **4. As a group, list four things you could do to learn more about this topic.**<br><br>Go to the library.<br><br>Rent a movie about it.<br><br>Talk to somebody who survived it.<br><br>Interview an ex-German soldier.<br><br>Look up old newspaper articles from that time. |
| **5. Imagine this topic doesn't exist or never existed. Describe two ways the world might be different. Ask the player on your right for help.**<br><br>There would be a lot more people around.<br><br>There would be no Holocaust museum.<br><br>Nazis wouldn't be so unpopular.<br><br>The Germans would have won the war. | **6. Compare learning about this topic to learning about something else, in or out of school. Ask any player for help.**<br><br>Learning about the Holocaust and learning about the bombing in Japan were both sick and sad.<br><br>I compared this to learning about endangered species; we read novels and saw movies. |

**Figure 5.4.** Fifth-grade students' responses to a Connection Cube game about the Holocaust.

## Topic: Colonial period

| 1. List two new ideas you have about this topic that you didn't have before studying it. | 2. Ask each player in the group to name one activity or job in which knowing about this topic could be important. |
|---|---|
| I didn't realize the colonists traded that much with Indians. I thought they were enemies.<br><br>I didn't know that many people died trying to settle America.<br><br>None of the colonists would have survived if they hadn't gotten *some* help from England. | Librarian<br>Art collector<br>Museum manager<br>Teacher<br>Antique dealer<br>People who work at Plymouth Plantation |
| **3. Make a connection between this topic and something else you know.**<br><br>The colonists were a lot like us because they understood that they needed to make laws to maintain society.<br><br>Colonial families and communities had to pull together just to survive. Families aren't like that now. | **4. As a group, list four things you could do to learn more about this topic.**<br><br>Go to Williamsburg or Plymouth Plantation.<br><br>Ask a parent.<br><br>Do research using CD-ROM disks.<br><br>Read the textbook.<br><br>Write to the Library of Congress. |
| **5. Imagine this topic doesn't exist or never existed. Describe two ways the world might be different. Ask the player on your right for help.**<br><br>We would not celebrate the Thanksgiving holiday.<br><br>We would still be ruled by the British.<br><br>The Indians would have united to settle the country. | **6. Compare learning about this topic to learning about something else, in or out of school. Ask any player for help.**<br><br>We use cooperative groups to learn about things in school the same way the colonists learned from the Indians.<br><br>We read from the textbook at first, like we did when we learned about the American Revolution. |

**Figure 5.5.** Fifth-grade students' responses to a Connection Cube game about the Colonial Period.

## Topic: Westward Movement

| 1. List two new ideas you have about this topic that you didn't have before studying it. | 2. Ask each player in the group to name one activity or job in which knowing about this topic could be important. |
|---|---|
| I didn't know the fur trade influenced the Westward Movement.<br><br>I didn't know the Oregon Trail was part of the U.S.<br><br>I had no idea what this topic was when we started it; now I wonder what the Indians thought about us moving west. | History teacher<br>Archeologist<br>Tourist<br>Any job, because it's supposed to be common knowledge<br>Historian |
| **3. Make a connection between this topic and something else you know.** | **4. As a group, list four things you could do to learn more about this topic.** |
| It's like the people on the Mayflower exploring new territory.<br><br>Lots of families got split up during the Westward Movement, like they did during the Civil War. | Take a trip along the Oregon Trail.<br><br>Go to the library.<br><br>Build a covered wagon.<br><br>Make maps of the territory.<br><br>Ask a teacher. |
| **5. Imagine this topic doesn't exist or never existed. Describe two ways the world might be different. Ask the player on your right for help.** | **6. Compare learning about this topic to learning about something else, in or out of school. Ask any player for help.** |
| We might not have settled Oregon and made it part of the Union.<br><br>We wouldn't have fought a war with Britain over it.<br><br>The U.S. would be smaller. | Learning this topic is like basketball because you have to practice both to get good at them.<br><br>Reminds me of the computer game we played when we learned about the Oregon Trail in fifth grade. |

**Figure 5.6.** Eighth-grade students' responses to a Connection Cube game about the Westward Movement.

## Topic: *A Day in the Life of Ivan Denisovich*

| | |
|---|---|
| **1. List two new ideas you have about this topic that you didn't have before studying it.**<br><br>I understand why the "gang bosses" might see prisoners as not being human, when of course, the prisoners really are.<br><br>That people tend to identify with groups. Even in the worst conditions, people want to belong to something. | **2. Ask each player in the group to name one activity or job in which knowing about this topic could be important.**<br><br>Prison guards<br>Members of Congress<br>School administrators<br>History teachers<br>Business managers<br>Journalists or reporters |
| **3. Make a connection between this topic and something else you know.**<br><br>The struggles the prisoners faced in the story are in many ways, the same struggles people face everyday at work or in school.<br><br>It reminded me of the World War II death camps we learned about in U.S. history class. | **4. As a group, list four things you could do to learn more about this topic.**<br><br>Read more about past and present-day Russian prison systems.<br><br>Ask a concentration camp survivor.<br><br>Ask a Russian historian.<br><br>E-mail the Library of Congress.<br><br>Go to the Holocaust Museum in Washington. |
| **5. Imagine this topic doesn't exist or never existed. Describe two ways the world might be different. Ask the player on your right for help.**<br><br>Atrocities of prison camps might still be going on.<br><br>We'd live in total anarchy.<br><br>The author would not have been "banished" for writing the story. | **6. Compare learning about this topic to learning about something else, in or out of school. Ask any player for help.**<br><br>This is like when we read *Night* by Eli Weisel to learn about the Jewish concentration camps.<br><br>It's kind of like reading Faulkner to learn about life down South. It's fiction, but you learn a lot about what southern life is like. |

**Figure 5.7.** Twelfth-grade students' responses to a Connection Cube game about *A Day in the Life of Ivan Denisovich.*

# *Where to Go from Here: Planning Future Lessons*

It is almost impossible to understand something too deeply. As long as students continue to actively construct new connections that broaden their web of knowledge, they will continue to deepen their understanding of a topic, no matter what the topic is. So making connections doesn't necessarily mark the end of the learning process. In many cases, it marks the beginning.

As you review students' work, the following questions can help you develop ideas about how to use the Connection Cube to plan or supplement future lessons:

- Do any areas suggested by students' connections invite further study or suggest interesting interdisciplinary investigations?

- What do the responses say about your students' level of understanding? What dimensions of their understanding need to be deepened?

- What connections or comments did students make about their own learning processes? In what ways was their learning strong? In what ways might their learning skills improve?

- What big themes emerged? How can these themes enrich future topics in the curriculum?

The following sample scenarios illustrate how future lessons can build on the Connection Cube. These scenarios are by no means prescriptions. The key to following up the Connection Cube is to let the themes or patterns of students' responses guide your lesson planning.

## Making Connections Between Art and Music

Mr. Ashworth, a music teacher, used the Connection Cube with his seventh-grade students. He noticed that many of the responses connected learning in art with learning in music. Not knowing exactly how to pursue this further, Mr. Ashworth decided to conduct a brainstorming activity with his students. Maybe some unifying theme or topic would emerge; perhaps he and the art teacher could pursue that topic together.

Mr. Ashworth asked his students to brainstorm all the connections they could between music and art. For the next 10 minutes, Mr. Ashworth's students filled the board with ideas. When they stepped back, they noticed a recurring theme: art and music share many terms and concepts, such as rhythm, structure, mood, and framing. This seemed like a really important connection! That afternoon, Ms. Ashworth and the art teacher got together to discuss how they might capitalize on them in their teaching.

## Identifying Relevance for History Class

Ms. Raymond was a history teacher in an inner-city high school. She frequently commented that her greatest challenge was making her subject relevant to her students' lives. Always looking for creative ways to bring history into the present, Ms. Raymond decided to use the Connection Cube in the middle of a unit on immigration. She wanted to push her students to identify one or two important political or social themes that were meaningful to them and that they could explore in depth as they covered other topics and historical events throughout the year.

During a follow-up discussion, the class discovered that the concepts of justice and fairness tied together many historical and current events. Ms. Raymond listed on the board the main topics the curriculum would cover that year and asked students to work in small groups to brainstorm ideas for exploring the concepts of fairness and justice as they related to each topic. Ms. Raymond sat in on groups as they worked and recorded their ideas in her notebook.

# 6

# The
# Reflection
# Cube Game

## How the Reflection Cube Cultivates Critical Thinking and Understanding

Our minds are truly remarkable. Not only are we amazing learning machines, capable of such feats as making difficult decisions and solving complex problems, we also have the ability to stand back and reflect on our own thinking.

In recent years, psychologists have used the term *metacognition* to label the cognitive processes involved in thinking about thinking. They have argued that metacognition is a key component of intelligence; by this they mean that effective thinking involves the ability to reflect on and evaluate one's own thinking and learning processes. In school settings, research has shown over and over again that metacognition is a *learnable* component of intelligence: Students who are taught to be more reflective about their own thinking do a better job of learning and understand the topics they are studying.

Education is, of course, no different than other fields: Good ideas stand the test of time, but often their labels change. Educators from Socrates on have recognized the importance of reflection. Most recently, psychologists have introduced the term *self-regulated learning* to refer to the way metacognition enhances self-directed, self-evaluative learning. Despite the changing labels, the research findings remain the same: Reflective learners tend to learn more effectively and understand topics more deeply.

The Reflection Cube offers a cognitive strategy for helping students to be more reflective and self-evaluative about their own learning. Drawing on the research about metacognition and self-regulation, the questions on the Reflection Cube are designed to cultivate critical thinking and understanding in the following ways:

- **Thoughtful self-critique.** The Reflection Cube asks students to thoughtfully evaluate the learning they just did by identifying both its strengths and its weaknesses and by formulating advice for others who will study the topic.

- **Identifying and reviewing big messages.** Too often, students don't have an opportunity to review and revisit what's important to them about what they've learned. The Reflection Cube cultivates understanding by providing an opportunity for students to sum up the big messages about the topic they've just studied.

- **Exploring learning preferences and tendencies.** The Reflection Cube invites students to explain, with reasons, what aspects of the learning they enjoyed most and least. This helps students to develop a better understanding of their own learning tendencies, which in turn helps them to be better self-regulated learners.

- **Using the language of thinking.** The words we hear and use affect the way we think. Effective metacognition involves being able to use thinking-rich language to describe one's own thinking and learning processes. By asking students to brainstorm various words to describe their thinking, and by providing them with sample language, the Reflection Cube encourages students to use thinking-rich language to describe and discriminate among various kinds of thinking processes.

## *When to Use the Reflection Cube*

**Use the Reflection Cube at or near the end of a topic or unit.**

A good time to use the Reflection Cube is at the end of a topic or unit. The Reflection Cube challenges students to take a close look at the learning they have done. For this reason, it is important that studying the topic has involved more than rote memorization. For example, perhaps students have been writing essays or solving problems. Perhaps they have been applying knowledge to new contexts or working on an independent project. Maybe they have conducted experiments or research. All of these learning processes are worth exploring with the Reflection Cube.

**Use the Reflection Cube in the middle of a topic or unit after a particularly rich learning experience.**

Use the Reflection Cube when students have just completed a particularly meaningful learning experience, even if it occurs in the middle of a unit. For example, use the Reflection Cube after students have taken an important exam, after they've completed a project, after they've written an important essay, after they've studied a difficult chapter, or after they've learned a difficult concept. Reflecting on rich learning episodes like these helps students consolidate and anchor their new knowledge.

## *Getting Started*

1. Choose a Reflection Cube topic. It can be virtually any topic in any subject in any grade. The Reflection Cube asks students to reflect on the learning they just did, so the richer and more varied students' learning of the topic has been, the more interesting the game will be.

2. Schedule a time to play the game. Typically, the game is played at or near the end of a topic or unit. It takes about 15 minutes to play the Reflection Cube game. (See the When to Use the Reflection Cube section of this chapter for more suggestions about when to play the game.)

3. Have students work in small cooperative groups. Give each group

   - a Reflection Cube game piece, pre-assembled or to assemble themselves (pattern appears in figure 6.1)

   - a Response Sheet (figure 6.2)

4. Explain the rules aloud, and either post the rules where students can easily refer to them, or give each group a copy of the rules. (See figure 6.3 for rules.)

5. Remind groups to record their responses on the Response Sheet as they play the game. Collect the sheets when the groups are done. If you wish, provide written or verbal feedback using the Guidelines for Feedback in this chapter.

6. See the Where to Go from Here section of this chapter for suggestions about how to build on the Reflection Cube in future lessons.

**1.**

Name two strengths in the thinking you just did.

**5.**

What did you enjoy most about the thinking you just did? What did you enjoy least? Why?

**3.**

Describe one way in which the thinking you just did could have been better.

**4.**

What advice would you give to someone who was about to do the activity or study the topic you just did?

**2.**

All players: Together, brainstorm a list of thinking words (investigate, create, analyze, etc.) that describe the thinking you just did. Time limit: 1 minute. (Roll again if the group has already done this.)

**6.**

All players: Together, brainstorm two or more big messages about the topic. List central ideas, important things to remember, interesting ideas or facts.

*To assemble: Cut along the solid lines, fold on the dotted lines, and tape together to form a cube.*

**Figure 6.1.** The Reflection Cube game piece.

From *Critical Squares: Games of Critical Thinking and Understanding.* © 1997.
Teacher Ideas Press 1-800-237-6124.

# Reflection Cube Response Sheet

Topic: _____

Names: _____

_____

Record your responses for each roll of the Reflection Cube. If the same challenge is rolled twice, just add the responses to the correct column.

---

**Challenge 1**

Name two strengths in the thinking you just did.

---

**Challenge 2**

All players: Together, brainstorm a list of thinking words (investigate, create, analyze, etc.) that describe the thinking you just did. Time limit: 1 minute. (Roll again if the group has already done this.)

---

**Figure 6.2.** Reflection Cube Response Sheet.

## Reflection Cube Response Sheet (continued)

**Challenge 3**
Describe one way in which the thinking you just did could have been better.

**Challenge 4**
What advice would you give to someone who was about to do the activity or study the topic you just did?

**Figure 6.2.** Reflection Cube Response Sheet (continued).

## Reflection Cube Response Sheet (continued)

**Challenge 5**

What did you enjoy most about the thinking you just did? What did you enjoy least? Why?

**Challenge 6**

All players: Together, brainstorm two or more big messages about the topic. List central ideas, important things to remember, interesting ideas or facts.

**Figure 6.2.** Reflection Cube Response Sheet (continued).

# *Rules of the Reflection Cube Game*

*For groups of 3–5 players.*

1. Players take turns rolling the die. Each player has one roll per turn. The player with the last birthday in the calendar year rolls first.

2. Roll the die and answer the thinking challenge that faces up. The player who rolls the die records his or her responses on the Reflection Cube Response Sheet.

3. Go around the circle twice, so each player has two turns.

4. Some questions ask the whole group to respond. For group challenges, the player who rolls the die records the group's responses on the Response Sheet.

5. Sometimes, the same thinking challenge comes up two times in a row. If this happens, the player or group must respond to the challenge again. If the challenge comes up more than two times in a row, roll the die again for a new thinking challenge.

**Figure 6.3.** Rules of the Reflection Cube game.

## Sample Student Responses

Review figures 6.4–6.7 to get a sense of what types of responses students give when they are asked to reflect on their own thinking. All of the responses in the student samples were produced by real students in regular school settings, and they relate to traditional curricular topics.

As you review the responses, notice the various ways which students articulate their ideas about how they monitor and manage their thinking. Some of their observations show more depth, sophistication, and insight than others. The samples in sum represent the range and quality of responses you can expect from your students when they use the Reflection Cube.

## Guidelines for Feedback: Responding to Students' Thinking

By design, playing the Reflection Cube game is itself a valuable source of feedback, because it challenges students to be reflective and self-evaluative about their own thinking and learning. Your job is to provide feedback about how effectively they are doing this. This requires a bit of mental gymnastics, because providing feedback on the Reflection Cube game means providing students with feedback about how well they are giving themselves feedback. But it is simpler than it sounds.

The four categories into which students' responses typically fall are:

- Thoughtful self-critique

- Identifying and reviewing big messages and key ideas

- Exploring thinking patterns, trends, and tendencies

- Using the language of thinking

Use these categories to focus the feedback you give students. Following are specific things to look for in each of these categories, along with some examples drawn from actual student responses.

### Thoughtful Self-Critique

Identify and commend questions or comments that indicate students noticed...

effective and ineffective thinking strategies; stronger or weaker areas of factual and process knowledge; areas of thinking that may need improvement; observations of learning strengths; how thinking met good thinking standards.

**Examples**

*Start the project early and keep a positive attitude.*

*A strength was I tried to think of something that* wasn't *good about the Endangered Species Act.*

*I could have taken more time to think about what exactly I wanted to say in my paper, instead of just writing the first thing I thought of.*

## Big Messages and Key Ideas

Identify and commend observations that show...

a sensitivity to the deeper meaning and themes embedded in the topics; personal and relevant connections to the content or process of learning.

### Examples

*The key to learning about the stock market is to learn what the codes stand for. I learned a lot after that.*

*I compared African cultures and values to our own.*

*I think it's cool that Africa used to be part of South America.*

## Exploring Patterns, Trends, Tendencies

Identify and commend responses that indicate students...

compared their thinking to the thinking they have done on other tasks; noticed things or dimensions that influence the effectiveness of their thinking; detected a particular thinking trend over time; explained what they enjoyed most or least about their thinking and learning.

### Examples

*I felt rushed. I did not have enough time to think of a good project.*

*Planning a science project is like writing a research paper; you need to get organized early.*

*I paid more attention to current events in Africa while we were doing this unit.*

*I feel like I learn better when I have to make some real project or thing.*

## Using the Language of Thinking

Identify and commend questions or comments that show that students...

used rich thinking language to precisely describe their thinking; used thinking vocabulary to distinguish various aspects of their understanding.

As you look for the language of thinking, look for words like *suggest, explain, describe, assume, imagine, investigate,* or *analyze.*

### Examples

*The way I **organized** the project could have been better. I took too long to do the research.*

*It's important to **consider** the **effects** of things (environment) on other species.*

*I was **surprised** when I saw the project from a whole new **perspective.***

## Topic: Endangered species of the United States

| | |
|---|---|
| **1. Name two strengths in the thinking you just did.**<br><br>I decided to go to the town library to look for other resources and materials for our presentation.<br><br>A strength was that I was trying to think of something that *wasn't* good about the Endangered Species Act. | **2. All players: Together, brainstorm a list of thinking words (investigate, create, analyze, etc.) that describe the thinking you just did. Time limit: 1 minute. (Roll again if the group has already done this.)**<br><br>Search<br>Conclude<br>Analyze<br>Wonder<br>Debate<br>Guess<br>Examine<br>Imagine |
| **3. Describe one way in which the thinking you just did could have been better.**<br><br>I could have accepted other people's ideas for the project better.<br><br>I could have taken more time to think about what exactly I wanted to say in my paper, instead of just writing the first thing I thought of. | **4. What advice would you give to someone who was about to do the activity or study the topic you just did?**<br><br>Know the difference between *endangered*, *threatened*, and *extinct*.<br><br>Use lots of visuals and photos in your presentation; don't just talk.<br><br>Find out if there's an endangered species in your area, and do your project on that. |
| **5. What did you enjoy most about the thinking you just did? What did you enjoy least? Why?**<br><br>Most: That I tried to think of ways people could live better without destroying wildlife habitat.<br><br>Least: When we had to write an outline before starting the project. I'd rather just do it. | **6. All players: Together, brainstorm two or more big messages about the topic. List central ideas, important things to remember, interesting ideas or facts.**<br><br>I never thought of wildlife as a resource that should be protected.<br><br>It's important for us as people to consider the effects of things on other species.<br><br>Extinction is final. |

**Figure 6.4.** Fifth-grade students' responses to a Reflection Cube game about endangered species of the United States.

## Topic: The stock market

| | |
|---|---|
| **1. Name two strengths in the thinking you just did.**<br><br>I asked lots of questions at first. I knew I didn't understand how the stock market worked.<br><br>We did some research before we started our project.<br><br>We have a better idea what we would do differently if we had to do this project again. | **2. All players: Together, brainstorm a list of thinking words (investigate, create, analyze, etc.) that describe the thinking you just did. Time limit: 1 minute. (Roll again if the group has already done this.)**<br><br>Speculate<br>Analyze<br>Predict<br>Forecast<br>Guess<br>Research<br>Evaluate<br>Consider |
| **3. Describe one way in which the thinking you just did could have been better.**<br><br>I overestimated how much I knew about money and banking from the last chapter.<br><br>Even though my project was good, I still don't *really* know about interest rates and how they affect stocks and bonds. | **4. What advice would you give to someone who was about to do the activity or study the topic you just did?**<br><br>Don't get behind; you'll have to learn tons of new terms, like *Consumer Price Index.*<br><br>Get a newspaper that has a daily business section with stock quotes in it, so you don't have to borrow one.<br><br>Try to watch the business segments of the nightly news, even if you don't understand all of it. |
| **5. What did you enjoy most about the thinking you just did? What did you enjoy least? Why?**<br><br>Most: I enjoyed predicting how well our companies were doing on the stock market and building our investment portfolio.<br><br>Least: I hated memorizing all the new vocabulary terms every night. | **6. All players: Together, brainstorm two or more big messages about the topic. List central ideas, important things to remember, interesting ideas or facts.**<br><br>The key is learning what all the codes and indexes stand for. I learned a lot after I got that.<br><br>I like being able to understand TV news better. Dow Jones and all that stuff isn't such a mystery now. |

**Figure 6.5.** Seventh-grade students' responses to a Reflection Cube game about the stock market.

## Topic: A science fair

| | |
|---|---|
| **1. Name two strengths in the thinking you just did.**<br><br>It was good practice for my brain.<br><br>I learned to cooperate and work with people within my group.<br><br>I thought of a lot of sources before I started the project. | **2. All players: Together, brainstorm a list of thinking words (investigate, create, analyze, etc.) that describe the thinking you just did. Time limit: 1 minute. (Roll again if the group has already done this.)**<br><br>Analyze<br>Design<br>Efficient<br>Creative<br>Investigate<br>Research<br>Committed<br>Artistic |
| **3. Describe one way in which the thinking you just did could have been better.**<br><br>The way I planned the project could have been better. I took too long to do the research.<br><br>I could have thought of a better topic. | **4. What advice would you give to someone who was about to do the activity or study the topic you just did?**<br><br>Start early and keep a positive attitude.<br><br>Do something useful, not just any old project.<br><br>Choose a topic that's at your own level.<br><br>Focus your project on something specific. |
| **5. What did you enjoy most about the thinking you just did? What did you enjoy least? Why?**<br><br>Most: I was surprised that I saw the project from a new perspective when I was done.<br><br>Least: Feeling rushed and not having enough time to think of a good project. | **6. All players: Together, brainstorm two or more big messages about the topic. List central ideas, important things to remember, interesting ideas or facts.**<br><br>Planning a science project is a lot like writing a research paper. You need to get organized early.<br><br>I feel like I learn the topic better when I have to make some real project or thing. |

**Figure 6.6.** Eighth-grade students' responses to a Reflection Cube game about a science fair.

## Topic: African geography

| | |
|---|---|
| **1. Name two strengths in the thinking you just did.**<br><br>I was able to relate the topic to books and news shows I've seen.<br><br>I compared African cultures and values to our own.<br><br>I paid more attention to current events in Africa while we were doing the unit. | **2. All players: Together, brainstorm a list of thinking words (investigate, create, analyze, etc.) that describe the thinking you just did. Time limit: 1 minute. (Roll again if the group has already done this.)**<br><br>Connect<br>Examine<br>Associate<br>Compare<br>Memorize<br>Create<br>Relate<br>Summarize<br>Investigate<br>Learn |
| **3. Describe one way in which the thinking you just did could have been better.**<br><br>Instead of memorizing, I would have tried to learn the material better.<br><br>I would have asked questions as soon as I didn't understand something during the discussion. | **4. What advice would you give to someone who was about to do the activity or study the topic you just did?**<br><br>Do some background reading on your own. The textbook is outdated.<br><br>Go into it with an open mind. Some of the topics are pretty interesting.<br><br>Take good notes. There's a lot of info to cover. |
| **5. What did you enjoy most about the thinking you just did? What did you enjoy least? Why?**<br><br>Most: That I was able to keep everything straight in my head for the test.<br><br>Least: We had to memorize a lot of material. We never got a feel for anything before we moved on to the next topic. | **6. All players: Together, brainstorm two or more big messages about the topic. List central ideas, important things to remember, interesting ideas or facts.**<br><br>I think it's cool that Africa used to be part of South America. I can't see how land shifted so much, and still is shifting!<br><br>A shift in climate or abuse of the land could easily turn the U.S. into a desert like the Sahara in Africa. |

**Figure 6.7.** Eleventh-grade students' responses to a Reflection Cube game about African geography.

# *Where to Go from Here:*
# *Planning Future Lessons*

Be sure to review the responses your students generated while playing the Reflection Cube game. Even the most cursory review of students' responses often reveals at least one or two promising, or in some cases problematic, patterns in students thinking that you might want to address with follow-up lessons or activities.

The patterns that emerge might indicate areas of weakness that warrant attention—a lack of understanding of the topic, superficial or unbalanced self-critique, or misconceptions of big themes or messages, for example. You may also notice positive trends emerging. Your students may have uncovered an interesting new theme connected to the topic; you may want to pursue this theme as a class. Or perhaps you will notice some thinking language creeping into students' responses; this may lead you to develop lessons that encourage students to use their new thinking vocabulary in other areas. Whatever the case, following are some questions to help you reflect on your students' experience:

- What was promising, interesting or surprising about students' comments?

- What patterns or big messages did you notice in the students' comments?

- What aspects of students' thinking might need improvement or attention?

Don't feel you must answer all of these questions formally. Just mull them over and think about what kinds of future lessons and activities they suggest.

To stimulate your thinking, following are two scenarios that illustrate how you might build on the Reflection Cube in planning future lessons.

## Identifying Key Ideas

After completing a unit on botany, Ms. Esposito's class played the Reflection Cube game. When she reviewed her students' responses later that night, she noticed that many students mentioned they learned the most about botany when they constructed their terrariums, because they had to do something, not just read about it. She knew that active learning deepens understanding, but she was surprised to see her students recognized it in their own learning, too. She then opened her plan book and brainstormed some ideas for hands-on projects she could introduce into her social studies lessons.

## Using Thoughtful Self-Critique

Mr. Paultz used the Reflection Cube after giving a trigonometry quiz. Upon review, he noticed something odd. He noticed students commented only about the negative tendencies of their thinking. Things like, "I can't think when I feel pressure on a test" or "My thinking bogs down when I can't remember the formulas." Almost no one commented on the positive aspects of their thinking, aspects that actually helped them think constructively through the quiz.

Mr. Paultz remembered a technique he had learned about in an inservice workshop called "One-Minute Papers." The workshop was about metacognition and about helping students to be more reflective about their own thinking and learning processes. The technique was as follows: After a quiz, ask students to take one minute to answer three simple questions: (1) What aspects of your thinking went well on this quiz? (2) What aspects of your thinking would you like to improve? and (3) What would you do differently next time you take a quiz like this? Mr. Paultz decided to give it a try, to have his students reflect on the positive, as well as the negative, aspects of their thinking.

# Bibliography

*Critical Squares* is one of several publications by research associates at Harvard University's Project Zero. For teachers interested in learning more about Project Zero's work on the theoretical and practical dimensions of critical thinking and understanding, we offer this annotated list of selected publications authored by Project Zero associates.

Blythe, Tina. With other associates of Project Zero and teachers of the Teaching for Understanding Project. In press. *Understanding Up Front: A Handbook on Teaching for Understanding.* New York: Jossey-Bass.

This book is intended for an audience of teachers and administrators learning to use the Teaching for Understanding (TfU) framework. Chapters on generative topics, understanding goals, understanding performances, and ongoing assessment define the vocabulary, offer practical models, and make suggestions for beginning to work with TfU. Understanding Up Front is an excellent resource for a study group.

Goodrich, Heidi, Tom Hatch, Gwynn Wiatrowski, and Chris Unger. 1995. *Teaching Through Projects: Creating Effective Learning Environments.* New York: Addison-Wesley.

Based on four years experience at the Mather School in Boston, this book gives teachers and other educators the tools they need to develop successful projects for their classrooms, after-school programs, and other educational settings. It includes a discussion of what makes a project and guides teachers in designing their own project-based curricula.

Perkins, David. 1995. *Outsmarting IQ: The Emerging Science of Learnable Intelligence.* New York: Free Press.

This book explores how contemporary efforts to teach better thinking challenge the traditional concept of IQ. Whereas the IQ tradition sees intelligence as fixed by genetic and other factors, a new science is emerging—the science of learnable intelligence—that allows anyone to become a more able and committed thinker and learner.

————. 1994. *The Intelligent Eye: Learning to Think by Looking at Art.* J. P. Getty Trust.

*The Intelligent Eye* presents an argument for the value of looking at art as a means to cultivate "thinking dispositions." Drawing on recent research in cognition, this volume explains why looking at art is uniquely qualified to support commitments to habits of thinking that deepen our understanding of specific works of art and at the same time strengthen our thinking and learning in other domains.

————. 1992. *Smart Schools: From Training Memories to Educating Minds.* New York: Free Press.

*Smart Schools* asks what we know about the art and craft of teaching and about the organization of schools that can help make schools more powerful and inspiring settings for learning. The books marshals findings from cognitive psychology and other areas, exploring both theory and practical implications around such themes as cultivating creative and critical thinking, teaching for understanding, and motivating students to welcome intellectual challenges.

———. 1986. *Knowledge as Design.* Hillsdale, NJ: Lawrence Earlbaum Associates.

*Knowledge as Design* is a general approach to teaching and learning the subject matters with an emphasis on thinking and understanding. The approach involves viewing virtually any topic—fractions, democracy, Newton's laws, the Boston Tea Party—as a design, something with a structure shaped to serve one or more purposes. Teachers and students think about and come to understand a topic by exploring its design elements.

Perkins, David, Heidi Goodrich, Shari Tishman, and Jill Mirman Owen. 1994. *Thinking Connections: Learning to Think & Thinking to Learn.* New York: Wesley.

*Thinking Connections* teaches thinking within the context of the regular curriculum. Designed for use across the curriculum with students of all ages, it teaches three thinking strategies: (1) mental management, a strategy for controlling and improving one's thought processes; (2) decision making, a strategy for making decisions and evaluating the decisions of others; and (3) understanding through design, a strategy for systematically achieving a deep understanding of almost anything—in or out of the classroom.

Remer, Abby, Shari Tishman, Heidi Goodrich, David Perkins, and others at Learning Designs. 1992. *The Thinking Teacher's Guide to the Visual Arts.* Produced by Learning Designs of New York City. GPN/University of Nebraska.

*The Thinking Teacher's Guide to the Visual Arts* is an educational resource for teachers using *Behind the Scenes,* a PBS television series on the arts. The curriculum combines a hands-on approach to the visual arts with the development of critical and creative thinking skills that are relevant to student learning in all subjects.

Swartz, Robert, and David Perkins. 1990. *Teaching Thinking: Issues and Approaches.* Midwest Publications.

This book provides an overview of the field of critical and creative thinking for the practitioner. *Teaching Thinking* helps teachers think through a number of important issues and questions concerning teaching thinking and provides guidance for determining which approaches are working and which are not.

Tishman, Shari, David Perkins, and Eileen Jay. 1995. *The Thinking Classroom: Learning and Teaching in a Culture of Thinking.* Boston: Allyn and Bacon.

*The Thinking Classroom* is a book about the teaching of thinking. It focuses on creating a culture of thinking in the classroom. Rich with examples, this book shows how educators can use cultural forces already present in the classroom to cultivate six dimensions of high-level thinking: language of thinking, transfer, thinking dispositions, the strategic spirit, higher-order knowledge, and metacognition.

Wiske, Stone, ed. In press. *Teaching for Understanding: A Practical Framework.* Developed and written by associates of Project Zero and Harvard University Graduate School of Education. New York: Jossey-Bass.

Geared to academic audiences, this book reports findings from a six-year research project at the Harvard Graduate School of Education and Project Zero. The book outlines the history and context of the project and explains the "performance" view of understanding. It introduces TfU (Teaching for Understanding), a four-element framework to help teachers become more reflective and intentional about their efforts to teach for understanding, and the understanding framework, which identifies four dimensions of understanding. Portraits of four teachers' efforts to learn the framework and the effects on their students are described and examined.

# Index

# About the Authors

**Dr. Shari Tishman** is a research associate at Harvard Project Zero at the Harvard University Graduate School of Education. Her work focuses on the theory and teaching of high-level cognition. She works with educators nationally and internationally on the development of thinking-centered instruction, and has written extensively about the teaching of critical and creative thinking.

**Albert Andrade** is a researcher at Harvard Project Zero at the Harvard University Graduate School of Education. His work at Project Zero centers on the theory and practice of teaching higher-order thinking and learning. He works frequently in schools, and his professional interests include developing instructional materials and designing thinking-centered curricula with and for teachers.

*from* Teacher Ideas Press

## CRIME SCENE INVESTIGATION
*Barbara Harris, Kris Kohlmeier, and Robert D. Kiel*

Clueless about how to generate classroom excitement? You won't be with this book. Students step into the roles of reporters, lawyers, and detectives at the scene of a crime. Participants build problem-solving skills as they examine clues, make a case, and bring it to trial. Detailed instructions and reproducibles are included. **Grades 5–12** *(adaptable to other grades).*
*xiii, 109p. 8½x11 paper ISBN 1-56308-637-9*

## WHAT A NOVEL IDEA!
### Projects and Activities for Young Adult Literature
*Katherine Wiesolek Kuta*

Designed around the new language arts standards (reading, writing, representing, viewing, speaking, and listening), these stimulating activities for novels create opportunities for students to develop skills and become better readers, writers, and speakers. **Grades 7–12.**
*xi, 143p. 8½x11 paper ISBN 1-56308-479-1*

## NATURE PUZZLERS
### Thinking Activities from the Natural World
*Lawrence E. Hillman*

Bring a little intrigue into the classroom with these puzzling anecdotes from the real world of nature. Written to encourage critical-thinking and problem-solving skills, they serve as springboards to activities across the curriculum—from active discussions to research projects, brainstorming, creative writing, and much more. **Grades 6–12.**
*xiv, 152p. 8½x11 paper ISBN 0-87287-778-7*

## TALENTED
### Strategies for Developing the Talent in Every Learner
*Jerry D. Flack*

"The best little resource for classroom teachers!" according to *Teaching K–8*, this book shows how all children can learn well and achieve excellence if provided with opportunity and challenge. Activities promote literacy, integrated learning, diversity, and academic excellence. **Grades K–12.**
***Gifted Treasury Series; Jerry D. Flack, Ed.***
*xiii, 249p. 8½x11 paper ISBN 1-56308-127-X*

## FROM THE LAND OF ENCHANTMENT
### Creative Teaching with Fairy Tales
*Jerry D. Flack*

Inspirational and practical, this book offers a wealth of ideas, curriculum, resources, and teaching techniques that promote multiple intelligences, critical thinking, creative problem solving, and product-based learning. Fairy tales provide a common theme to a variety of engaging activities such as making books, writing newspapers, and creating a classroom museum. **All levels.**
***Gifted Treasury Series; Jerry D. Flack, Ed.***
*xix, 241p. 8½x11 paper ISBN 1-56308-540-2*

**For a FREE catalog or to order these or any Teacher Ideas Press titles, please contact:**
**Teacher Ideas Press**
Dept. B9916 • P.O. Box 6633 • Englewood, CO 80155-6633
Phone: 1-800-237-6124, ext. 1 • Fax: 303-220-8843 • E-mail: lu-books@lu.com